Prime Time

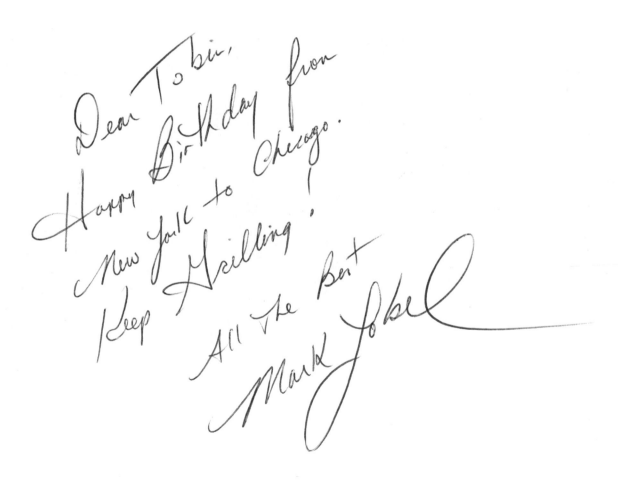

Dear Tobin,

Happy Birthday from
New York to Chicago.
Keep Grilling!

All The Best

Mark Jobel

Prime Time

THE LOBELS' GUIDE TO GREAT GRILLED MEATS

Evan, Leon, Stanley, and Mark Lobel

MACMILLAN · USA

MACMILLAN
A Pearson Education Macmillan Company
1633 Broadway
New York, NY 10019-6785

Macmillan Publishing books may be purchased for business or sales promotional use. For information, please write:
Special Markets Department, Macmillan Publishing USA, 1633 Broadway, New York, NY 10019-6785.

Cataloging-in-Publication Data is available from the Library of Congress

Printed in the United States of America

10   9   8   7   6   5   4   3

To my wife, Tamie. With her wisdom and support, I now know that I can climb any mountain I choose. Also to my children, Joey and Cori, for their unconditional love and understanding.

—Evan Lobel

To the future great cooks, my granddaughters: Stephanie Angel, Michele Angel, Rebecca Angel, Joanna Lobel, and Cori Lobel; and to any future grandchildren to come, with all my love. Every time you are cooking or grilling I will be there with you—Your Pops.

—Leon Lobel

To my dear wife, Evelyn, my partner in life who makes each day brighter for me than the day before; to my wonderful sons, David and Mark, of whom I am so very proud; my lovely daughters-in-law, Carla and Christine; and my little rewards, Brian, Jessica, Vicki, and Erika, with enormous love and devotion. Thank you God for blessing me. Thank you Mom and Dad.

—Stanley Lobel

To my dear wife, Carla, my best friend and inspiration in life; to my little love Brian, who brings so much joy and laughter into my life; and to my wonderful parents, Evelyn and Stanley, whose love and support are endless. You all mean the world to me.

—Mark Lobel

"The Lobel family is known to most of us for their wondrous assorted meats and fowl. But did you know that all of them pride themselves with their cooking skills?

The recipes in this grilling book are really excellent, tasty, easy, and foolproof—if you follow the directives, which are clearly explained.

I look forward to many evenings grilling outdoors."

—**Martha Stewart**

Contents

Acknowledgments

It is impossible to thank everyone who contributed to this book: our respective families and friends who offered encouragement and advice along the way; our clientele who enthusiastically asked when "our next book" was coming out; our employees who happily put in a little extra time while we worked on the manuscript. But there are a few people we would like to thank personally, for without them this would be a very different—and not nearly as good—book:

Mary Goodbody who worked closely and caringly with us to shape the words and recipes into a coherent, readable manuscript.

Susan Lescher who brought us to Macmillan.

Jim Willhite who took great care seeing our manuscript through the editorial process. Deborah Callan, Francine Fielding, and Elizabeth Wheeler who helped so much with the recipes.

Finally, we want to thank our loyal customers who, over the years, have made it possible for us to run the kind of shop where the art of butchery is practiced still, and where true quality meat and poultry, as well as dedication to service, are appreciated. Without you, there would be no Lobel's.

Introduction

For us, grilling is a family affair. Not only do we come from a long line of butchers, but we come from a long line of accomplished cooks with a love of meat—and what better way to cook meat than on the grill? Obviously, our grandfathers didn't have the efficient outdoor grills that we do today, but from the day we tasted our first grilled steak, we were hooked. Undoubtedly, our grandfathers and great-grandfathers would have been, too.

There are four names on the front of this book, which represent two brothers and a son of each. Leon and Stanley learned the butcher business from their father, Morris, and have, in turn, taught it to their sons, Evan and Mark. All four of us relish good food and the enjoyment that comes with its preparation and serving, and nowhere do we get more of this pleasure than when we stand in our own (or each other's) backyards and man the grill.

Why We Love to Grill

Above all, we consider grilling good fun. If it's not, something is wrong. It's a joyous type of cooking if ever there were one. The aroma of the smoke alone signals a good time. When meat or poultry is sizzling on the grill, everyone gathers around, eagerly anticipating the meal to come.

For the grill cook, it's as important to feel relaxed and loose as it is to tend properly to the food. For this, we usually find ourselves with a few friends by our sides and a glass of wine or bottle of beer nearby, although a tall glass of iced tea or lemonade is as welcome. The point is to enjoy the process and never consider it a chore. Kick back! Have fun! It's a party!

Nevertheless, grilling is a serious method of cooking. It's important to know how to build a good fire and maintain the heat, when to cover the grill and when to use it as a brazier (open grill). The finest meat you can buy is prime. If you can acquire it, it will unquestionably taste better than other meat. However, because prime meat is dear, it must be treated with respect both before and during grilling. Of course, once it's off the grill, it's every man for himself.

We explain at the opening of each chapter how to select and then handle the meat or poultry, and later, in individual recipes, offer our best advice for grilling success. In the opening chapter of the book on page 1, we discuss different grills, how to build a fire, how to maintain the heat, and what tools you will need. In short, how to conquer the logistics of being a backyard grill warrior. But also remember that grilling, like all types of cooking, is personal. Once you find the style that appeals to you, go with it. The more often you fire up the grill, the better you will get at it. No fire, whether fueled by charcoal or gas, burns exactly the same. Every grill is a little different, and so cooking times will vary. The weather plays a role, too, in determining the intensity of the fire. We have been "grill meisters" for decades and still learn something new every season.

Why We Wrote This Book

All four of us love to grill. We appreciate expertly prepared meat and poultry and want to share our knowledge. However, equally important to us is that grilling signals family time. Sunday afternoon, for example, is a great time for an outdoor get-together with loved ones. These parties are the ideal events to gather old and new friends, invite children and grandparents, fill a cooler with soda and beer, and then fire up the grill in anticipation of great eats. Grilling is most fun in the warm weather, but even if the mercury drops, grilling a whole chicken or rack of lamb outdoors can turn an indoor meal into a casual, festive occasion.

Over the years we have noticed obvious changes in our customers' buying habits. Thirty years ago, customers bought far more roasts, stewing meats, and other large cuts; today, they buy steaks, ground meat, chops, boned chicken breasts, and pork loins. Our informal customer surveys (those we conduct over the counter as we wrap up the meat for our customers) inform us that, during the summer, at least seventy-five percent of these purchases end up on a grill. This indicates to us that grilling is the cooking method of the future.

Such an observation makes sense. As Americans have less and less time for cooking, it's natural for grilling to take center stage. It's quick and easy, with little cleanup. It also lends itself to advanced preparation in terms of marinating or rubbing the meat with spices. These techniques also beckon to the creative cook in all of us. An increasing number of our customers rely on gas grills, which are as easy to ignite as a gas stove. Others are loyal to hardwood charcoal, while still others prefer grilling indoors on a stovetop grill, particularly if the weather is uninviting.

Any and all methods of grilling make sense to us. We simply love to grill.

How We Became Butchers

We almost had no choice. We come from generations of men in the meat business, beginning with our great-grandfather who with his son, our grandfather, ran beef cattle near Czernowitz, which was part of the Austrian Empire from 1775 to 1918. Our grandfather added a slaughterhouse to the business and because he knew so much about cattle in general, was able to apply this knowledge to the art of butchering. His son, Morris, learned the business from him so that by the time he was 14 years old, he was buying and selling his own cattle. At the age of 17, Morris, like so many other young men of that era, emigrated to the United States to start life in the New World.

Morris's career began in Boston. He eventually found his way to New York where he established a butcher business, first in the Bronx and later on the Upper East Side of Manhattan, where we still do business today at 1096 Madison Avenue, near the corner of East Eighty-second Street. We wonder if Morris would recognize the business as it is run today. Granted, aged prime meat still hangs in the meat locker, but there are cooked meat and poultry dishes for sale. These include whole roasted chicken and beef stew—and smaller cuts ready for smaller families and the changing needs of the modern-day cook. We also market our own bottled barbecue sauce, which, as we do meat, we sell on our website as well as in the store. Clearly this is marketing for the twenty-first century.

This is how we think it should be. We pass our knowledge on to our children, who in turn incorporate it even as they evolve the business to meet the demands of the times. But one thing never changes. We understand and revere good butchering.

Butchering is a lost art. Today, meat is butchered at the wholesale location, wrapped in Cryovac (air-tight plastic) and shipped to its destination. Hanging meat for aging seems to be a thing of the past, except among a small group of butchers. Aging itself is an art and can mean the difference between a good- and a great-tasting piece of meat. We respect these traditions and deliberately take the best of the old and combine it with the requirements of the present and future. For example, all our meats are aged and all are cut to our customers' specifications and needs.

We believe it is crucial to treat our customers fairly and pleasantly, to sell only quality meat, and to answer every question. Because of this dedication to our customers, we have grown and changed, and along the way have learned even more about meat and meat cookery. This is knowledge we have happily shared with customers and with anyone else who asks.

Our customers are among the most famous and influential people in the world. We have advised private chefs and restaurant chefs on how to cook our prime meat for world leaders, captains of industry, glamorous film stars, artists, and Broadway legends. But the majority of our customers are our neighbors, people who appreciate good meat and good service and with whom we have developed warm and lasting relationships over the years. We would like this book to become an extension of just this sort of relationship. Once you begin cooking from it and gain a greater understanding both of your backyard grill and how best to prepare meat and poultry, we truly hope you will come to think of us as butchers and grill experts you can trust.

CHAPTER 1

LOBEL'S EYE VIEW
OF GRILLING BASICS

Before the grill, before the fuel, before the perfect summer afternoon, you need good meat. This is our first and most important caveat: Buy the best you can afford, handle it with care, and then, when the fire is hot enough, when the meat has been allowed to reach cool room temperature, and when you are starting to get hungry, carefully lay it on the grill rack and anticipate an outstanding meal. Our second caveat is: Use a grill you enjoy and trust.

Various grill experts tout the virtues of a particular kind of grill. We admit to having our favorites, but when you get right down to it, what you have or what you like is the best grill for you. Make sure the grill is large enough, that neither the grill rack nor the firebox is rusted, and that you are comfortable cooking on it. If these criteria are not met, perhaps it is time to consider buying a new grill. For instance, there's no good reason to hold onto a flimsy tabletop grill with short, stubby legs if you would be more at ease with a waist-high, standing grill.

Grills

Some aficionados swear by brazier-style grills with racks that can be raised or lowered, but we prefer grills with covers and stationary (but removable) grill racks. By removing the cover, you can use the grill as a brazier and by replacing the lid, you can raise the temperature of the cooking chamber and thus affect the cooking time. Opening and closing the vents in the lid can influence cooking temperatures, too.

Covered grills can be round or rectangular. Very few are equipped with racks that move up and down, so all food is cooked about six inches from the fire. We tested the recipes in this book with such grills. We have observed that a majority of grills available at hardware stores and the large discount chains are either covered grills, hibachis, or inexpensive table-top grills—the sort you might take to the beach that are next to useless for serious grilling.

With covered grills, the grill lids trap the smoke, which infuses the food with outdoorsy flavor, while at the same time smothering flare-ups. Most covered grills have vents, or dampers, on both the top of the lid and the bottom of the grill, making it easy to control the heat. If the fire is burning too slowly, open a bottom vent to add a little oxygen to feed the fire. If the food is cooking too quickly, open a top vent to allow some heat to escape.

The most popular covered grill is the kettle-style grill, which is round with a domed lid that, rather than being hinged, lifts off completely. The round kettle reflects and deflects the heat evenly, which is particularly advantageous when you are cooking large pieces of meat such as turkeys, standing rib roasts, or even whole chickens.

Covered grills are small and large, with some table-top models suitable for balcony or boat-deck grilling. With these versatile grills, you can cook over direct heat or not, depending on how you arrange the coals. You can sear the meat on the open rack, marking it nicely with grid lines and sealing in the juices, and then cover the grill to keep the fire hot and the food cooking evenly. At the end of cooking, remember to remove the lid so that the meat develops a crispy crust.

Hibachis are small, Japanese-style brazier grills that are generally well made and just about perfect for some grilling needs. If you have a small backyard and a small family, you will not go wrong with a hibachi for many grilling needs. These approximately 10 × 15-inch iron grills are excellent for grilling steaks, chops, and chicken breasts that need hot, direct heat. For success, lay the pieces of food close together on the grill rack so that they nearly touch and, therefore, cover the rack almost completely to hold in heat. When the party is over, move the hibachi to a protected place—it will rust in the rain.

Gas grills are growing in popularity and as they do, their prices are dropping, although they still cost significantly more than other grills. Even as we confess to a slight preference for charcoal grills because of the flavor imparted to the food, we grill on gas grills all the time. Why? They are so convenient! A gas grill essentially is an outdoor gas stovetop. The fire is lit and the heat is controlled by the turn of a knob, and because there are always two burners, and sometimes three, it is an easy matter to move food to the "cool part of the grill" for slow cooking. You just turn one burner down or off. Gas grills never burn quite as hot as the hottest charcoal fire, but they reach temperatures more than adequate for backyard grilling needs.

Gas grills can be extremely fancy, with multiple burners, warming baskets, rotisseries, and even side gas burners suitable for saucepans for keeping the sauce warm or boiling the marinade. Others are pretty basic: two burners and removable grill racks.

Some gas grills are connected to the main gas line coming into the house, making them as ready to use as the kitchen stove. These often are built into the patio or deck as a feature for an outdoor kitchen, a concept that is growing in popularity as the population moves to the Sunbelt. Other gas grills are fueled by canned propane. The propane is inexpensive—usually you can get the can refilled at a local gas station or hardware store—and one can lasts for seven or eight hours of grilling. For some folks, this means only one or two fill-ups during a summer, while for others (like us!) it can mean multiple trips to the gas station. We have two cans that fit our grills and keep the second one filled and on hand in case the first one runs out while the turkey is roasting or the burgers are sizzling.

Fuel

Charcoal grills need charcoal, and when you meander down the supermarket aisle these days you may be astounded by the variety available. This is good news because it means it is now easy to buy our fuel of choice, hardwood lump charcoal, which also may be called natural charcoal. We like it because it burns hotter, longer, and cleaner than standard briquettes, and although it is irregularly shaped and so a little clumsy to use, we go for it every time. These lumps are made from hardwoods, such as oak, maple, cherry, mesquite, and hickory. Some people wrongly assume that burning mesquite or hickory hardwood charcoal will give their grilled food a distinctive flavor. On the contrary, these charcoals may smoke a little more than other types of coal, but any imparted flavor will be subtle at best.

If a noticeable woody flavor is your goal, buy hardwood chunks. These are nothing more complicated than simple wood—not wood that has been compressed into charcoal. The wood requires a good forty or forty-five minutes to get hot enough for grilling, burns more quickly than charcoal, and never reaches the same high temperatures—but the flavor of the wood is easily discernible on the food without being unpleasant. Wood also produces more smoke than charcoal. For these reasons, charcoal is generally the favorite fuel of the back-yard chef. Experimenting with wood, however, can be fun.

None of this is to say that standard briquettes are not good fuel. They are evenly shaped and less expensive than hardwood lump charcoal—two attributes that many folks appreciate. But they burn more quickly and a little cooler than hardwood lump charcoal, so you may need more briquettes if you are grilling for any length of time—such as cooking a roast or large whole chicken. However, unless you buy the super-duper discount special (the cheap-est you can find), standard briquettes burn evenly and cleanly.

We do not recommend self-lighting briquettes, which are saturated with chemicals so that they ignite with a match as easily as a wad of newspaper. This convenience product imparts an unappetizing oily flavor to the food. The manufacturer may claim that the chem-icals "burn off" once the charcoal reaches cooking temperatures, and while many do, we can't help but notice a residual flavor—even if it's only in our imaginations.

We also caution against cheap charcoal. It burns "dirty," partly because it has been made with fillers such as second- or third-rate sawdust, and it also burns quickly, so you will need more, which can quickly counteract any financial savings.

Like wood chunks, wood chips provide real wood flavor. However, these cannot be con-sidered fuel, but merely flavoring agents. They may be labeled "smoking chips" and com-monly are from woods such as oak, cherry, maple, aspen, hickory, apple, and—the all-time favorite—mesquite. The small pieces of wood, sold in venues ranging from gourmet special-ty markets to hardware stores, smoke just enough to give food a mild, smoky flavor. The chips must be soaked in water to cover for twenty to thirty minutes before they are scattered over the hot coals to produce a good smoke cloud. Too many chips can dampen the fire or extinguish it completely, so use wood chips judiciously. Also, it's important to use only recommended hardwoods for chips or for chunks—soft woods such as pine, spruce, or cedar produce billows of bitter, acrid smoke.

Water-soaked fresh herb sprigs, citrus peel, and cinnamon sticks also can be used to make aromatic smoke. However, don't expect any of these smoke makers to flavor the food very much. They are no replacement for spice rubs and marinades. But they make the air smell wonderful and enhance the entire grilling experience—which is why we love them.

Building and Lighting the Fire

When figuring on the number of coals you will need for most grilling, estimate that about five pounds of standard briquettes or three or four pounds of hardwood lump charcoal is ade-quate. Another way to figure this amount is to spread the briquettes in a single layer in the firebox so that the surface area is slightly larger than that of the food. If you will be grilling for longer than 30 or 40 minutes, you will need to add six or seven fresh coals to the fire to maintain the temperature every twenty-five or thirty minutes after that time.

There are several ways to light coals. One of the most popular is to use a chimney. To use these sturdy, inexpensive metal cylinders, pile the charcoal in the larger, top section of the chimney, stuff crumbled newspaper in the bottom and light the paper. The coals ignite as the heat from the paper fire sweeps up the chimney. When the top briquettes are barely covered with gray ash, pour them into the firebox and spread them out or stack them for indirect cooking.

Electric starters are effective, too, although the grill must be close to an electric outlet. The looped heating element is attached to a heatproof handle. To use, spread briquettes in the firebox, lay the electric starter over them, and then pile more briquettes over it. In a very short time, the coals near the starter will be smoldering. Remove the starter and push the coals into a mound until all are covered with gray ash.

You can also use solid starters, which are small blocks of pressed wood fibers that are saturated with flammable chemicals and ignite quickly. Unlike self-lighting briquettes, the amount of flammable chemicals is so tiny that the starters impart no unpleasant flavors.

Liquid starter, or charcoal lighter fluid, is the most popular ignition agent in America. If not used correctly, it is a backyard accident-waiting-to-happen. To use a liquid starter, pile the briquettes in the center of the firebox and douse with the lighter fluid. Let the fluid permeate the coals for about one minute, and then light the coals in several places with long safety matches. When the coals are covered with gray ash, spread them out for grilling. Some people complain that liquid starters make the food "taste funny," but in fact, the starters burn off long before the coals are ready and no residual flavor remains. However, they do smell oily while they are burning, which may be the cause for the complaint.

Liquid starters turn dangerous when impatient grill chefs squirt them onto already hot coals to "speed up the process" or if they are not sure the coals actually ignited. Too often this results in scary flare-ups and perhaps singed eyebrows, or worse. For this reason, never let children use liquid starters.

Direct and Indirect Grilling

You may be perplexed by these terms, although they are quite logical. Because the heat of a grill cannot be regulated by the turn of a knob as it can on the stove, backyard cooks have come up with two basic ways to cook: on hot grills and on not-so-hot grills. It's as simple and sensible as that, and as you become accustomed to your grill and your own likes and predispositions, you will probably find yourself using these methods or combinations of them without really thinking about them.

For most grilling, the ignited coals are spread in a single layer under the food. This is called direct grilling. The single layer of coals emits even, steady heat, whether the grill is open or covered, and represents the way most people grill. For more control, pile some of the coals at one side of the grill where they will emit intense heat. You can move the food around on the grill, setting it over the very hot coals when you want to sear it or when a thick piece needs to cook a little more quickly.

For some grilling needs, you will want to use indirect grilling. This method is for long, slow cooking in a covered grill, and when it is appropriate, it is indicated in the recipes. For indirect cooking, the coals are piled two or three coals deep on one side of the grill, or divided and piled on two sides. This leaves an empty space next to the coals or between them. Food cooked over indirect heat often is started over direct heat and then moved to the cooler (empty) part of the grill for even, slow cooking. To make the heat as even as possible, construct two piles of coals.

Many grill cooks place a metal drip pan in the empty space beside or between the coals, which is filled with water, wine, beer, broth, or a combination. Set the food directly over the drip pan. These inject a little extra moisture into the cooking environment and also catch dripping juices and fat, which makes cleanup a little easier and reduces the chance of flare-ups. (Remember to keep a spray bottle filled with water on hand to extinguish flare-ups.) Generally, we don't use drip pans, finding them cumbersome and irrelevant except in very specific instances, but you may want to try them.

When grilling on a gas grill, you only have to turn off one of the burners for indirect grilling and keep the other burner(s) at medium or high. Do not prepare the gas grill for indirect grilling by preheating only one burner. Let the grill preheat with all burners on high as usual, and then turn one or two off.

Once you get used to the indirect method, you may prefer to use it for more grilling tasks than we specify in the recipes. Although it may take a little longer, it is an excellent cooking style and a sure way to prevent the food from burning and to promote even cooking.

The Heat of the Fire

In our recipes we call for the coals to be "hot," "moderately hot," or, most often, "moderately hot to hot." Occasionally, we call for "moderately cool" coals. There is a graphic at the top of each recipe specifying the heat of the fire, too—just in case you miss it in the recipe! But what do these terms mean?

The Heat of the Coals

	seconds you can hold the palm of your hand 4 inches above the coals	temperature range (°F)	visual cues
HOT COALS	2	400 to 450	barely covered with gray ash; deep red glow
MODERATELY HOT TO HOT COALS	3	375 to 400	thin coating of gray ash; deep red glow
MODERATELY HOT COALS	4	325 to 375	significant coating of gray ash; red glow
MODERATELY COOL COALS	5	300 to 325	thick coating of gray ash; dull red glow

No doubt you have read grilling books and pamphlets that talk about gray ash and the red glow of the coals. These are valid visual descriptions. Hot coals are those that are barely covered with gray ash and are deeply glowing red underneath. Moderately hot to hot coals are covered with a thin layer of gray ash and are glowing deep red. Moderately hot coals are covered with a little more gray ash and still glow. Moderately cool coals are covered with a thick layer of gray ash and are glowing only slightly. With hot coals, you can hold the palm of your hand four inches above them for only two seconds before it feels uncomfortably hot—for moderately cool coals you can hold the palm of your hand over the coals for a full five seconds.

Thermometers

We think instant-read meat thermometers are one of the greatest inventions for the backyard grill cook. It's reassuring to know that the interior of the chicken has reached 170°F for white meat, or the pork is indeed 150° to 155°F, which means it will reach 160°F after it rests for a few minutes and will be thoroughly cooked without being dry. And when the interior of the steak is 130°F, you feel confident that the meat will be gloriously rare and juicy. These thermometers are sold in hardware and cookware stores and through cooking catalogs, are made of sturdy metal or plastic, and have a sharp point for inserting in the meat.

Internal Temperatures for Meat and Poultry

chicken:	170°F for white meat
	180°F for dark meat
turkey:	170°F for white meat
	180°F for dark meat
pork:	160°F; cook until temperature is 150 to 155°F and then let the meat rest for 5 to 10 minutes. The internal temperature will rise to 160°F but the meat will not be overcooked.
lamb:	140°F for rare meat
	150°F for medium meat
	160°F for well-done meat
beef:	130°F for rare meat
	140°F for medium-rare meat
	150°F for medium meat
	160°F for well-done meat

Many gas grills and some of the high-end charcoal grills are fitted with thermometers to gauge the interior temperature of the cooking chamber. Grilling is not an exact science, and so the precise temperature of the coals or cooking chamber is not as crucial as it might be for a culinary activity such as baking. If your grill does not have a thermometer, do not despair. We like the visual cues and open-hand test described on page 7 as much. However, place an accurate oven thermometer under the lid of a covered grill, or insert a thermometer through the vents in the lid to read the temperature if it gives you more confidence.

Other Equipment

Grill manufacturers gladly will sell you any number of accessories for the outdoor grill, and for anyone who likes gadgets, collect them to your heart's content. But for the rest of us, there are only a few pieces of equipment that are almost crucial.

Every backyard chef should have long-handled tongs, spatulas, and forks with heatproof handles, as well as several long-handled, soft-bristle brushes for brushing marinades and sauces on the meat. Of these essentials, the least important is the fork, because it's usually inadvisable to pierce the meat and release juices. Turn it with spatulas and tongs, if possible, and use the fork for other tasks. We also like mesh grill screens, which can be laid on the grilling grid and used to grill delicate foods, such as ground-chicken burgers.

Also invest in long, heavy oven mitts and, as previously mentioned, an accurate instant-read thermometer. With good, sharp knives, which every good cook likes to have, and large cutting boards, that's about it.

We also suggest you stock the kitchen with shallow glass or ceramic dishes for marinating or with several large rectangular, inflexible plastic containers with tight-fitting lids, or both. Heavy-duty plastic bags with zipped closures are handy for marinating, too.

For kabobs, have six or more ten- to twelve-inch-long metal skewers. Bamboo skewers, which are inexpensive and can be bought in packages of twenty or more, are great, too, although they need to be soaked in cold water for at least twenty minutes before use so that they won't smolder on the grill. These can be short for appetizer-sized kabobs, or longer for entree kabobs. The short wooden skewers are useful for skewering chickens and quail when preparing them for the grill.

It is important to keep the grill and the grill rack clean. For this, you'll need a stiff metal bristle brush for scrubbing the rack. Scouring pads are also good for keeping the racks clean. If you aren't too busy enjoying the meal, clean the grill rack while it is still warm—any burned-on food will come off easily. Spraying the grill rack with vegetable oil cooking spray keeps the food from sticking and so helps with cleanup.

The firebox does not need frequent scrubbing, although the built-up ashes should be cleaned out and the inside periodically sprayed clean with a hose and left to dry in the sun or wiped dry with paper towels.

A Word on Food Safety

It is just as important to maintain sanitary conditions when cooking meat and poultry outside as it is in the kitchen. Clean the cutting board and all utensils that have been in contact with uncooked meat or poultry with warm soapy water. Wash your hands, too, after working with uncooked food (chicken, in particular) to avoid salmonella bacteria.

Many grill cooks slather the grilling meat or chicken with its marinade. This is not a good idea except during the very early stages of cooking. The marinade can contain bacteria from the raw meat and poultry, and the heat of the fire will not have time to render the bacteria harmless if the marinade is brushed on the food in the final stages of grilling.

Grilling is a casual and relaxing way to cook and entertain. Once you have the basics in hand, don't worry. Half the fun is improvising when necessary—but the best part is eating the delicious food that comes from your grill.

BURGERS

Hamburgers are an American summertime tradition. But thanks first to diners and now fast-food restaurants, they are also a symbol of what many people don't know about quality meat. Truth be told, a good burger can be as good as it gets when it comes to casual dining—juicy and tender, bursting with robust meat flavor. On the other hand, an inferior burger can be a disappointing meal at best.

Most people buy ground meat in the supermarket, reserving the butcher shop for the "better" cuts. But we think it's far wiser to buy ground meat from a reliable butcher. When you walk into the butcher shop or approach the meat counter in a larger store, don't buy the ground meat on display, particularly if you have not developed a relationship with the butcher. That meat can be ground from any part of the animal, including trimmings. It's far better to ask the butcher to grind the meat for you, first trimming the fat before he puts it through the meat grinder. Let him know you will be using the meat for grilled burgers and ask him to grind it quite fine so that it can be formed into compact patties. If you buy preground, packaged beef or other meat, make sure it is rosy colored, without browned sections, and evenly mixed with creamy white particles of fat.

Beef is the most popular ground meat although we urge you to try lamb, veal, pork, turkey, and chicken, too. Ground meats other than beef and lamb do best when mixed together. When you experiment with other ground meats you will be happily rewarded with new taste experiences as well as expanded choices when it's time to eat!

The secret to successful grilled burgers is to make the patties firm and large so they neither fall apart on the grill nor slip through the grill rack onto the smoldering coals. As mentioned, evenly ground meat helps, as do bread crumbs and other ingredients added to the meat. Some of our burgers are nothing but lightly seasoned meat, others incorporate more ingredients. Also, to avoid crumbly burgers, open your fingers slightly when handling the meat; don't squeeze the meat and try not to overhandle it.

It's also important that the fire is hot enough before you put the burgers on the grill, and that the grill rack is lightly sprayed with vegetable oil cooking spray. These are important for all grilling, but particularly for burgers. Nothing ruins a burger faster than its bottom layer staying behind on the grill. And your mood won't be great, either, when you have to scrape the charred mess off the grill rack. Both a hot fire and an oiled grill prevent this. During grilling, turn the meat only once. If you flip flop the burgers (as you would a thin steak), they run the risk of crumbling.

We suggest cooking burgers until they are medium—although chicken, turkey, and pork burgers should be cooked until medium-well. Some folks like rare beef burgers and if you feel confident about the source of your meat, you can still enjoy them red and juicy in the center. However, as a rule, it's better to cook them until they are at least pink all the way through to be sure that any harmful bacteria have been killed. Use an instant-read thermometer to determine if the burgers are cooked. For beef, we like rare or medium-rare meat, but the USDA recommends well done. For pork, it should register 150° to 155°F, and for all poultry it should be at least 160°F.

Keep in mind that grilling is an inexact science—even more so than cooking on a stove. The heat of the fire will vary from grill to grill and depend, among other things, on the fuel you use and the ambient temperature of the day. Use the times provided in the recipes as guides. Our burgers may be fatter or rounder than yours and, therefore, will take longer. Once you know your own grill and your style of cooking, you will be able to determine the time it takes to cook the perfect burger perfectly.

Grilled burgers are great on their own, but you can load them onto lightly grilled or toasted hamburger rolls, Kaiser rolls, or any soft bun. Top them with red onions, lettuce, garden-fresh tomatoes, ketchup, flavored mayonnaises, bold salsas (see page 170 for some great mayonnaise and salsa recipes), mustard, or anything else you particularly like, and then sit back and enjoy the exquisite delight of a really great burger.

Storing and Grilling Ground Meat

Store ground meat in the refrigerator. As with all meat, do not unwrap it and rewrap it in your own plastic wrap or wax paper. Doing so exposes the meat to the air unnecessarily. If it is leaking, wrap an overlay of paper over the butcher's wrap. Meat is best stored in the rear of the lowest shelf of the refrigerator, which for most refrigerators is the coolest spot. Nevertheless, plan to cook the ground meat within one day of purchase.

Uncooked ground meat freezes well. Put the meat, still in its store wrapping, in a freezer-quality plastic bag, extract as much air as possible from the bag, and freeze the meat in the back of the freezer until frozen solid. After it is solid, you can shift it around in the freezer to make room for new additions. For more on freezing ground and other meat, see page 112.

Form the meat into patties and then grill them as soon as you can. Unlike other meat, successful burgers do not depend on the meat reaching room temperature before grilling. In fact, we advise seasoning and forming the chilled meat into burgers and then refrigerating it again before grilling, which helps keep the burgers from crumbling.

Using Vegetable Oil Cooking Sprays on Grill Racks

It's a good idea to grease grill racks so that the meat does not stick to them, making it easier to turn and move the meat around on the rack. A well-oiled grill makes cleanup easier, too. Be sure to oil the grill rack before lighting the fire to avoid flare-ups. (Keep a spray bottle of water nearby when you grill to extinguish flash fires.)

We have found that pressurized vegetable oil cooking sprays are efficient for the task of grilling. They are inexpensive, easy to use, and can be kept with the rest of the grilling tools so that they are always on hand. However, if you prefer, brush the grill with oil, using a broad-bristle brush or wadded-up paper towels.

Ground Beef Explained

Buy high-quality ground beef. We think ground chuck is the best for burgers, although we like the flavor of burgers made with a combination of chuck and sirloin or round. However, when you have to choose between one or the other, go for chuck. In every burger recipe, we instruct you to refrigerate the formed patties "until ready to grill." This is important, even if the refrigeration is only for 10 or 15 minutes. Room-temperature ground meat runs the risk of falling apart on the grill. The formed patties can be refrigerated for as long as four or five hours. Regardless of the type of ground meat, avoid overhandling; otherwise, the meat can toughen up.

Ground beef comes from various parts of the beast:

Ground chuck is from the forequarter

Ground round is from the rump

Ground sirloin is from the hindquarter

Grinding Your Own

To ensure that you get the best possible ground meat, grind your own at home. Trim the meat of all fat (including chicken skin) and grind it in a food processor fitted with a metal blade just until finely ground. (A food processor, as opposed to a meat grinder, can pulverize the meat, so take care that it does not become too mushy.) If you have a meat grinder, pass the meat through the grinder three times until finely ground.

Most butchers will grind the meat for you if you buy a whole cut. Ask yours to trim the fat before grinding the meat. Be sure to tell him you want the meat finely ground so that it will be easy to form into juicy burgers.

When Americans think hamburger, they think beef. We agree. Very little surpasses a great grilled beef burger—there are times when nothing else hits the spot. For the best, juiciest burgers, we suggest combining equal weights of ground sirloin and ground chuck. The only other cuts of beef we think should be ground are round and tail of porterhouse. Both can be used for burgers, but should be mixed with chuck. Hanger steak also makes great ground beef, but is hard to find. When working with ground beef, handle the meat gently to avoid toughening.

Classic Hamburger   *Serves 6*

1 POUND GROUND BEEF SIRLOIN

1 POUND GROUND BEEF CHUCK

SALT AND FRESHLY GROUND BLACK
    PEPPER TO TASTE

VEGETABLE OIL COOKING SPRAY

BAJA-STYLE TOMATO SALSA (PAGE 185)
    (OPTIONAL)

1. Combine the beef and salt and pepper in a bowl. Using your hands, mix well. Form into 6 patties. Refrigerate until ready to grill.

2. Prepare a charcoal or gas grill. Lightly spray the grill rack with vegetable oil cooking spray. The coals should be hot.

3. Grill the burgers for about 5 minutes. Turn and grill for 4 or 5 minutes longer for medium-well burgers. Serve with the salsa, if desired.

This is simply our Classic Hamburger with Cheddar cheese melted over it. We combine ground sirloin and chuck because we believe a great burger needs the fat in the chuck for juiciness and the quality of the sirloin for tenderness and flavor.

Cheddar Cheese Burgers *Serves 6*

1 POUND GROUND BEEF SIRLOIN

1 POUND GROUND BEEF CHUCK

SALT AND FRESHLY GROUND BLACK
   PEPPER TO TASTE

VEGETABLE OIL COOKING SPRAY

3 OUNCES SHARP CHEDDAR CHEESE,
   CUT INTO 6 UNIFORM SLICES

1. Combine the beef and salt and pepper in a bowl. Using your hands, mix well. Form into 6 patties. Refrigerate until ready to grill.

2. Prepare a charcoal or gas grill. Lightly spray the grill rack with vegetable oil cooking spray. The coals should be hot.

3. Grill the burgers for about 5 minutes. Turn and place a slice of cheese on top of each burger. Grill the burgers, covered, for 4 to 5 minutes longer until the cheese melts and the burgers are medium-well.

variation: **Pepper Jack Cheese Burgers:** Use 3 ounces of Pepper Jack cheese, sliced into 6 slices, in place of the Cheddar cheese.

Depending on the type of blue cheese you prefer, you may not be able to slice the cheese into firm slices. Most blue cheese crumbles and you will have to scatter the crumbled cheese over the burgers. Blue cheese melts nicely and its flavors blend seductively with the beef and the onions.

Blue Cheese Burgers with Grilled Onions *Serves 6*

1 POUND GROUND BEEF SIRLOIN

1 POUND GROUND BEEF CHUCK

SALT AND FRESHLY GROUND BLACK
    PEPPER TO TASTE

SIX ¹/₂-INCH-THICK SLICES WHITE
    ONIONS

VEGETABLE OIL COOKING SPRAY

CANOLA OIL

3 OUNCES BLUE CHEESE, CUT INTO 6
    SLICES OR CRUMBLED

1. Combine the beef and salt and pepper in a bowl. Using your hands, mix well. Form into 6 patties. Refrigerate until ready to grill.

2. Prepare a charcoal or gas grill. Lightly spray the grill rack with vegetable oil cooking spray. The coals should be hot.

3. Brush the onion slices with oil and season each with salt and pepper. Grill on the outer edge of the grill for 5 or 6 minutes until the onions begin to soften. Turn and grill for 8 or 9 minutes on the other side or until tender and lightly browned. Lift from the grill, set aside, and keep warm.

4. Grill the burgers for about 5 minutes. Turn and place a slice of cheese or crumble about ¹/₂ ounce cheese on top of each burger. Grill the burgers, covered, for 4 to 5 minutes longer, or until the cheese melts and the burgers are medium-well. Top with the onions and serve.

We love the idea of putting the cheese inside the burger, rather than on top of it. Make this with chuck alone for a juicier burger, although if you opt for sirloin alone, the cheese-mushroom filling will provide some moisture.

Stuffed Cheeseburger Deluxe   *Serves 6*

1 OUNCE DRIED MUSHROOMS (SEE
NOTE)

1/2 CUP VERY HOT WATER

1 POUND GROUND BEEF SIRLOIN

1 POUND GROUND BEEF CHUCK

2 TABLESPOONS WORCESTERSHIRE
SAUCE

2 TEASPOONS DRIED MARJORAM

2 TEASPOONS FRESHLY GROUND BLACK
PEPPER

4 OUNCES GORGONZOLA CHEESE,
CRUMBLED

4 SCALLIONS, FINELY SLICED

1 TEASPOON SALT

VEGETABLE OIL COOKING SPRAY

1. Put the mushrooms in a small bowl and add about 1/2 cup very hot water. Set aside for about 20 minutes for the mushrooms to hydrate.

2. Combine the beef, Worcestershire sauce, marjoram, and pepper in a bowl. Set aside.

3. Squeeze the mushrooms dry and discard the soaking liquid or reserve it for another use. Mince the mushrooms and combine the mushrooms with the cheese, scallions, and salt. Divide the cheese mixture into 6 equal portions, flattening each into a thick patty.

4. Divide the meat into 12 portions and flatten each into a patty. Set a cheese patty on 6 of the beef patties and top with the remaining beef patties. Press the edges of the patties closed to seal tightly and hold in the juices during grilling. Refrigerate until ready to grill.

5. Prepare a charcoal or gas grill. Lightly spray the grill rack with vegetable oil cooking spray. The coals should be moderately hot to hot.

6. Grill the burgers for about 5 minutes. Turn and grill for 4 or 5 minutes longer for medium-well burgers. Use a large spatula when turning the burgers, taking care that they do not split.

note: Dried mushrooms are sold in packages containing several different kinds. This mixture works well here, or buy loose dried mushrooms.

For this burger, which has become what we call a "pub favorite" in America, we again combine ground chuck with ground sirloin. If you prefer, you can use one or the other, but remember that sirloin alone will be a little drier than the combination. However, the bacon, although cooked, and the mushrooms add a little moisture. The chuck alone will produce a juicy and plump burger, but will lack a little of the deep flavor of the sirloin.

Bacon-Mushroom Burger   *Serves 6*

6 SLICES BACON (ABOUT 3 OUNCES)
1 POUND GROUND BEEF SIRLOIN
1 POUND GROUND BEEF CHUCK
¼ CUP PLUS 2 TABLESPOONS
    CHOPPED ONION
¼ CUP PLUS 2 TABLESPOONS
    CHOPPED WHITE MUSHROOMS
SALT AND FRESHLY GROUND BLACK
    PEPPER TO TASTE
VEGETABLE OIL COOKING SPRAY

1. Cook the bacon over medium heat in a skillet until cooked but not crispy. Drain on paper towels and when cool enough to handle, tear or chop into small pieces.

2. Combine the beef, bacon, onion, mushrooms, and salt and pepper in a large bowl. Using your hands, mix well. Form into 6 patties. Refrigerate until ready to grill.

3. Prepare a charcoal or gas grill. Lightly spray the grill rack with vegetable oil cooking spray. The coals should be hot.

4. Grill the burgers for about 5 minutes. Turn and grill for 4 or 5 minutes longer for medium-well burgers.

Sausage varies wildly in quality and seasonings. Buy your favorite hot Italian sausage from a butcher or shop you know and like. If you prefer, use another kind of sausage meat, flavored as you prefer, but use the best money can buy.

Spicy Sausage Burgers   *Serves 6*

10 OUNCES GROUND BEEF CHUCK

1/2 POUND GROUND BEEF SIRLOIN

3/4 POUND HOT ITALIAN SAUSAGE MEAT

SALT AND FRESHLY GROUND BLACK
   PEPPER TO TASTE

VEGETABLE OIL COOKING SPRAY

1. Combine the beef, sausage meat, and salt and pepper in a bowl. Using your hands, mix well. Form into 6 patties. Refrigerate until ready to grill.

2. Prepare a charcoal or gas grill. Lightly spray the grill rack with vegetable oil cooking spray. The coals should be hot.

3. Grill the burgers for about 5 minutes. Turn and grill for 4 or 5 minutes longer for medium-well burgers.

Ground veal should be from the shank, neck, or shoulder, because these cuts are moist and sweet flavored. Veal is lovely grilled and lends itself to gentle seasonings—and even when formed into burgers, retains its elegance.

Veal-Mushroom Burgers *Serves 6*

1 TABLESPOON OLIVE OIL

1¼ CUPS FINELY CHOPPED WHITE
   MUSHROOM CAPS

1 LARGE CLOVE GARLIC, MINCED

SALT AND FRESHLY GROUND BLACK
   PEPPER TO TASTE

2 POUNDS GROUND VEAL

2 TABLESPOONS CHOPPED FLAT-LEAF
   PARSLEY

VEGETABLE OIL COOKING SPRAY

ROASTED RED PEPPERS IN OLIVE OIL
   (PAGE 203)

1. Heat the olive oil in a skillet over medium-high heat. Add the mushrooms and cook, stirring, for about 1 minute, or until they begin to soften. Add the garlic and salt and pepper and cook for 2 or 3 minutes, or until the mushrooms soften. Set aside to cool.

2. Combine the veal, parsley, cooled mushroom mixture, and salt and pepper in a large bowl. Using your hands, mix well. Form into 6 patties. Refrigerate until ready to grill.

3. Prepare a charcoal or gas grill. Lightly spray the grill rack with vegetable oil cooking spray. The coals should be moderately hot.

4. Grill the burgers for about 8 minutes. Turn and grill for about 6 minutes longer for medium-well burgers. Serve with the red peppers.

When you buy ground lamb, ask that it be ground from the shoulder or shank. A mixture of these cuts is great, too. Ground lamb has enough body and flavor to stand on its own—no need to mix another ground meat with it—although we love seasonings such as garlic and rosemary.

Lamb-Rosemary Burgers *Serves 6*

2 POUNDS GROUND LAMB

2 TABLESPOONS DIJON MUSTARD

4 TEASPOONS CHOPPED FRESH
    ROSEMARY

1 TEASPOON MINCED GARLIC

1 TEASPOON SALT

$1/2$ TEASPOON FRESHLY GROUND BLACK
    PEPPER

VEGETABLE OIL COOKING SPRAY

1. Combine the lamb, mustard, rosemary, garlic, salt, and pepper in a large bowl. Using your hands, mix well. Form into 6 patties. Refrigerate until ready to grill.

2. Prepare a charcoal or gas grill. Lightly spray the grill rack with vegetable oil cooking spray. The coals should be hot.

3. Grill the burgers for about 7 minutes. Turn and grill for about 6 minutes longer for medium-well burgers.

Ground lamb can be mixed with all manner of flavorings, including piquant kalamata olives, and still taste very much like lamb. You can cook the onions and garlic in a skillet in the kitchen or, if you have a gas grill with a burner, cook them outside.

Greek Lamb Burgers   *Serves 6*

1 TABLESPOON OLIVE OIL

1 CUP DICED ONION

1 LARGE CLOVE GARLIC, MINCED

2 POUNDS GROUND LAMB

2 TABLESPOONS CHOPPED FLAT-LEAF
   PARSLEY

2 TABLESPOONS CHOPPED KALAMATA
   OLIVES

1 TABLESPOON CHOPPED FRESH MINT

MINTED SUMMER FRUIT SALSA
   (PAGE 183)

VEGETABLE OIL COOKING SPRAY

1. Heat the olive oil in a skillet over medium heat. Add the onions and cook for about 2 minutes, or until they begin to soften. Add the garlic and cook for 2 or 3 minutes longer, or until the onions are tender. Set aside to cool.

2. Combine the lamb, parsley, olives, mint, and cooled onions in a large bowl. Using your hands, mix well. Form into 6 patties. Refrigerate until ready to grill.

3. Prepare a charcoal or gas grill. Lightly spray the grill rack with vegetable oil cooking spray. The coals should be hot.

4. Grill the burgers for about 7 minutes. Turn and grill for about 6 minutes longer for medium-well burgers. Serve with the salsa.

Mixing ground turkey with ground pork produces a juicy, flavorful burger that is not overpowered by the pork. By itself, pork is too strongly flavored for burgers.

Spicy Southwestern Pork-Turkey Burgers

Serves 6

1 1/4 POUNDS GROUND TURKEY BREAST

3/4 POUND GROUND PORK

1/3 CUP CHOPPED RED PEPPERS

1/4 CUP CHOPPED SCALLIONS

1/4 CUP CHOPPED CILANTRO

1 JALAPEÑO, SEEDED AND CHOPPED

1 TABLESPOON PLUS 1 1/2 TEASPOONS
    CHILI POWDER

1 TEASPOON GROUND CUMIN

1 TEASPOON SALT

1/4 TEASPOON FRESHLY GROUND BLACK
    PEPPER

VEGETABLE OIL COOKING SPRAY

BAJA-STYLE TOMATO SALSA (PAGE 185)
    OR SOUTH-OF-THE-BORDER
    TOMATILLO SALSA (PAGE 184)

1. Combine the turkey, pork, peppers, scallions, cilantro, jalapeño, chili powder, cumin, salt, and pepper in a large bowl. Using your hands, mix well. Form into 6 patties. Refrigerate until ready to grill.

2. Prepare a charcoal or gas grill. Lightly spray the grill rack with vegetable oil cooking spray. The coals should be hot.

3. Grill the burgers for about 10 minutes. Turn and grill for 7 to 10 minutes longer for medium-well burgers. Serve with a salsa.

A common complaint from customers is that ground turkey breast is dry and tasteless. We agree that it needs moisture, which is why we often combine the turkey with another ground meat and other ingredients. Here, the apples provide flavorful moisture, while the bread crumbs help hold it in the meat. Mixing the turkey with ground veal helps, too. Serve these with Herbed Mayonnaise (page 202) or Chunky Cranberry Catsup (page 187).

Turkey-Veal Apple Burgers   *Serves 6*

1¼ POUNDS GROUND TURKEY BREAST

¾ POUND GROUND VEAL

½ CUP FRESH WHITE OR WHOLE WHEAT BREAD CRUMBS

1 FIRM, RIPE APPLE, CORED BUT NOT PEELED AND DICED

2 TABLESPOONS CHOPPED FRESH THYME

1 TEASPOON CHINESE FIVE-SPICE POWDER

1 TEASPOON SALT

1 TEASPOON WHITE PEPPER

VEGETABLE OIL COOKING SPRAY

1. Combine the turkey, veal, bread crumbs, apple, thyme, five-spice powder, salt, and pepper in a large bowl. Using your hands, mix well. Form into 6 patties. Refrigerate until ready to grill.

2. Prepare a charcoal or gas grill. Lightly spray the grill rack with vegetable oil cooking spray. The coals should be hot.

3. Grill the burgers for 8 to 10 minutes. Turn and grill for 5 to 7 minutes longer for medium-well burgers. The juices will run clear when the burgers are pressed gently with a spatula.

Ground turkey is showing up more and more in butcher shops and supermarket meat departments. When buying it, make sure it's ground from turkey breast. However, as healthful as ground turkey may be, it tends towards dryness. Here, the lemon juice adds a little moisture while accentuating the turkey's mild flavor. Moist hands help when forming these patties, as does well-chilled meat.

Turkey-Sage Burgers   *Serves 6*

2 POUNDS GROUND TURKEY BREAST

4 TEASPOONS CHOPPED FRESH SAGE

1 TABLESPOON FRESH LEMON JUICE

2 TEASPOONS CHOPPED FRESH THYME

SALT AND FRESHLY GROUND BLACK
   PEPPER TO TASTE

1. Combine the turkey, sage, lemon juice, thyme, salt, and pepper in a large bowl. Using your hands, mix well. Form into 6 patties. Refrigerate until ready to grill.

2. Prepare a charcoal or gas grill. Lightly spray the grill rack with vegetable oil cooking spray. The coals should be hot.

3. Grill the burgers for 6 to 8 minutes. Turn and grill for 5 to 7 minutes longer for medium-well burgers. The juices will run clear when the burgers are pressed gently with a spatula.

These turkey burgers may be a little more complicated to make than the others, but the zucchini and leek enhance the flavor of the turkey while providing needed moisture. Ground turkey, which is wet when raw, benefits from refrigeration before it is formed into firm patties, but that is not absolutely necessary if the other ingredients are chilled. Moist hands keep the meat from sticking so that the patties are easier to form. Try these with Baja-Style Tomato Salsa (page 185).

Turkey-Zucchini Burgers

Serves 6

1 CUP TIGHTLY PACKED, COARSELY GRATED ZUCCHINI (ABOUT 1 MEDIUM-SIZED)

SALT

1 TABLESPOON OLIVE OIL

1 SMALL LEEK, WHITE PART ONLY, HALVED LENGTHWISE AND SLICED CROSSWISE ¼ INCH THICK (SEE NOTE)

½ CUP FRESH BREAD CRUMBS (SEE NOTE)

2 TO 3 TABLESPOONS CHICKEN BROTH

1¼ POUNDS GROUND TURKEY BREAST

3 TABLESPOONS THINLY SLICED FRESH CHIVES

⅛ TEASPOON FRESHLY GRATED NUTMEG

FRESHLY GROUND BLACK PEPPER TO TASTE

VEGETABLE OIL COOKING SPRAY

1. Put the zucchini in a colander and salt lightly. Mix well and set aside for about 20 minutes, or until it begins to give up its juices. Quickly rinse the zucchini and let it drain, squeezing the moisture from it by the handful. When quite dry, press together into a mass and squeeze again to extract any remaining moisture.

2. Heat the oil over medium heat in a small skillet. Add the leek and sauté for about 5 minutes, or until softened. Add the zucchini and cook, stirring, for 5 or 6 minutes longer until the zucchini strands separate and any remaining excess moisture evaporates. Remove from the heat and set aside to cool until lukewarm.

3. Add the crumbs and broth to the vegetables and mix well.

4. Combine the turkey, chives, nutmeg, salt, and pepper in a bowl and mix lightly. Add the vegetable-bread crumb mixture and using your hands, mix thoroughly, being careful not to overmix the meat. Cover and refrigerate for about 1 hour until firm.

5. Form the turkey mixture into 6 patties. Refrigerate until ready to grill.

6. Prepare a charcoal or gas grill. Lightly spray the grill rack with vegetable oil cooking spray. The coals should be hot.

7. Grill the burgers for 8 to 10 minutes. Turn and grill for 5 to 7 minutes longer for medium-well burgers. The juices will run clear when the burgers are pressed gently with a spatula.

note: Leeks must be cleaned thoroughly or they may be gritty. For this recipe, halve lengthwise and soak in a sink of cold water for at least 10 minutes. Drain and rinse well. To make fresh bread crumbs, process fresh slices of bread in a blender or food processor. We particularly like French- or Italian-style baguettes for crumbs.

Similar in spirit to our Stuffed Cheeseburger Deluxe, this all-turkey burger is moistened by the bread crumb stuffing. Be sure the edges of the burgers are well sealed so that the moisture does not seep out the sides.

Stuffed Holiday Turkey Burgers with Chunky Cranberry Catsup   *Serves 6*

1 SCANT CUP FRESH WHITE OR WHOLE
   WHEAT BREAD CRUMBS

$1/3$ CUP CHOPPED FLAT-LEAF PARSLEY

$1/4$ CUP CHOPPED CELERY LEAVES

3 SCALLIONS, THINLY SLICED

2 TABLESPOONS UNSALTED BUTTER,
   MELTED

$1 1/2$ TEASPOONS POULTRY SEASONING
   (SEE NOTE)

$1 1/2$ TEASPOONS FENNEL SEEDS

1 TEASPOON CHOPPED FRESH THYME

SALT AND FRESHLY GROUND BLACK
   PEPPER TO TASTE

2 POUNDS GROUND TURKEY BREAST

VEGETABLE OIL COOKING SPRAY

CHUNKY CRANBERRY CATSUP
   (PAGE 187)

1. Combine the bread crumbs, parsley, celery leaves, scallions, butter, poultry seasoning, fennel, and thyme in a bowl. Mix well and season with salt and pepper. Form the stuffing into 6 small patties, each about $2 1/2$ inches in diameter.

2. Divide the turkey into 12 portions and flatten each into a patty. Set a stuffing patty on 6 of the turkey patties and top with the remaining turkey patties. Press the edges of the patties closed to seal tightly to hold in the juices during grilling. Refrigerate until ready to grill.

3. Prepare a charcoal or gas grill. Lightly spray the grill rack with vegetable oil cooking spray. The coals should be moderately hot to hot.

4. Grill the burgers for 6 to 8 minutes. Turn carefully and grill for 5 to 7 minutes longer for medium-well burgers. The juices will run clear when the burgers are pressed gently with a spatula. Serve with the Chunky Cranberry Catsup.

note: We used Bell's Poultry Seasoning, which is easy to find in supermarkets.

Ground chicken is perhaps the trickiest ground meat to form into burgers because it is so wet and mushy. Chill the meat well—or even partially freeze it—and work with moistened hands to prevent sticking. Because chicken can be so sticky, it helps to cook the burgers on a lightly oiled mesh grill screen that you set directly on the grilling grid.

Chicken Provençal Burgers   *Serves 6*

2 POUNDS GROUND CHICKEN BREAST

¼ CUP DIJON MUSTARD

¼ CUP DRAINED CAPERS (SEE NOTE)

¼ CUP CHOPPED FLAT-LEAF PARSLEY

2 SHALLOTS, CHOPPED

2 TABLESPOONS HERBES DE PROVENCE
   (SEE NOTE)

1 TEASPOON SALT

½ TEASPOON FRESHLY GROUND BLACK
   PEPPER

VEGETABLE OIL COOKING SPRAY

MUSTARD SAUCE (PAGE 182)

1. Combine the chicken, mustard, capers, parsley, shallots, herbes, salt, and pepper in a large bowl. Using your hands, mix well. Form into 6 patties, placing each on a small piece of waxed or parchment paper for easier transfer to the grill. Refrigerate until ready to grill.

2. Prepare a charcoal or gas grill. Lightly spray the grill rack with vegetable oil cooking spray. The coals should be hot.

3. Grill the burgers for 8 to 10 minutes. Turn and grill for 7 to 9 minutes longer for medium-well burgers. Serve with the Mustard Sauce.

note: Because the chicken is so moist, it's important that the other ingredients be dry. Drain the capers and pat them dry between sheets of paper towels. Herbes de Provence are available in supermarkets, but if you cannot find them, use dried oregano or thyme, or a mixture of the two. If the chicken seems too moist and you are afraid the patties will break when they are transferred to the grill, put them in the freezer for no longer than 30 minutes to firm but not to freeze them solid.

The mild flavors of chicken and veal complement each other, and the veal provides the naturally wet chicken with needed stability.

Chicken-Veal Burgers *Serves 6*

2 TABLESPOONS CANOLA OIL

1/2 TEASPOON DRIED ROSEMARY

1/2 TEASPOON FINELY CHOPPED ONION

1 TEASPOON CHINESE FIVE-SPICE
  POWDER

2 TABLESPOONS FINE DRIED BREAD
  CRUMBS

2 TABLESPOONS HARVEY'S BRISTOL
  CREAM (OPTIONAL)

SALT AND FRESHLY GROUND BLACK
  PEPPER TO TASTE

1 POUND LEAN GROUND CHICKEN

1 POUND LEAN GROUND VEAL

VEGETABLE OIL COOKING SPRAY

1. Combine the oil, rosemary, onion, five-spice powder, bread crumbs, and Bristol Cream in a large bowl and mix well. Season with salt and pepper.

2. Add the chicken and veal and using your hands, mix well. Form into 6 patties. Refrigerate until ready to grill.

3. Prepare a charcoal or gas grill. Lightly spray the grill rack with vegetable oil cooking spray. The coals should be hot.

4. Grill the burgers for 6 to 8 minutes. Turn and grill for about 5 to 8 minutes longer for medium-well burgers.

CHAPTER 3

BEEF AND VEAL

ithout question, beef is the favorite red meat for the grill. In our opinion, it is the best of all meat to grill and apparently backyard chefs across the nation agree, because beef accounts for nearly forty-five percent of all meat (including poultry) sold in the country. Granted, much of the beef tossed on the grill is in the form of ground chuck, patted into burgers, but who can deny the glory of a grilled sirloin or perfectly marinated flank steak? For those of us who appreciate high-quality red meat, just the term "char-grilled steak" can set our mouths to watering.

For the retail consumer, most beef is sold as *prime* or *choice*, grades of beef that denote certain qualities. Other grades exist. These are *good, standard, commercial, utility, cutter,* and *canner*. However, few retailers sell any grade below good. Grades are based on tenderness, juiciness, flavor, and cutability (the amount of useable meat on the carcass). Beef is also graded from one to five for cutability.

At our New York City shop, we sell only prime beef. Considering that only one or two percent of the beef produced in the country makes the grade of prime, you can be sure of getting premium beef when you shop at Lobel's. However, most Americans are not our customers! Ask your butcher what grade meat he sells and if you are lucky, he will say prime. However, choice beef is excellent and if that is what you can get, there is no need to be disappointed. In fact, Angus beef is choice beef. The top twelve percent of the choice-graded beef is Angus—beef from black Angus cattle. The stocky, short-legged black cattle have become a symbol for great steak (some Angus is sold under the brand name "Black Angus").

When shopping for beef at the supermarket, look for the words prime or choice on the label (you probably will not find prime meat in the supermarket). Look for a cut without an excessive amount of outer fat but with good, even marbling (streaks of fat). The marbling should not be heavy. The fat should look creamy and moist—not yellowed or gray. The color of the meat should be a healthy-looking cherry red, not a deep, dark red, and it should be evenly hued, not two-toned. Even if the meat is wrapped in plastic, when you press it, the meat should feel firm and finely textured.

Meat is best when aged, although it is not always possible to determine how long a piece of meat in the supermarket has been aged. At our shop, we age meat for four to six weeks, holding it at 34° to 36° Fahrenheit in coolers with well-circulated refrigerated air. The beef that arrives at the retailers often has only been stored for six to ten days. This is another reason to buy your meat from a reputable butcher with whom you have developed a good relationship. If this is not possible, we suggest ringing the bell at the butcher's counter in the supermarket and asking the butcher who answers the call how long the beef has been aged. If you can, avoid meat that is too fresh.

Unlike beef, veal requires no aging. At our shop, we sell veal as fresh as possible. Veal is from calves, although most of it comes from animals that are about five months old and weigh 350 to 400 pounds. Younger calves, called "vealers" in the trade, are only eight to twelve weeks old and weigh 150 to 250 pounds. Their meat is nearly white, which explains why this tender, mild meat is sometimes described as "milk-fed." True milk-fed veal is rare; only the youngest calves qualify and these are hard to find.

Veal should not be marbled, as the animals do not grow large enough to develop much fat. For this same reason, many cuts of veal are not ideal for grilling; there is not enough fat to keep the meat moist during the fast, dry-heat cooking of grilling. In this book we grill thick veal chops and cut veal sirloin or loin for brochettes, and we mix ground veal with other ground meat in the burger chapter, but otherwise we leave veal for slower indoor cooking, or quick sautéing.

Because the quality of veal must be superior, it is a good idea to buy it from a butcher you know. Regardless of its age, veal meat should be white or very light pink. It should look firm, moist, and velvety, and its soft bones should be red, appearing full of blood. While there will be no noticeable marbling, the thin layer of exterior fat should be white.

Preparing Beef and Veal for Grilling

When you get the meat home from the butcher or supermarket, immediately stow it in the coldest part of the refrigerator, which usually is the rear of the lowest shelf. Do not unwrap it; you do not want it to be exposed to the air unnecessarily and keeping it wrapped in its original packaging is a good idea.

When you are ready to prepare the beef—whether you are marinating it or grilling it virtually unadorned—take it from the refrigerator and let it come to room temperature, which means leaving it on the counter for about thirty minutes, still wrapped. If it is a particularly hot, humid summer day, reduce the counter time. Pat the meat dry with paper towels and then either marinate it, rub it with dry rub, or otherwise prepare it for the grill. We have not instructed you to pat the meat dry before marinating, rubbing, or otherwise preparing it in every recipe because it is universally appropriate whenever beef, veal, poultry, lamb, or pork is grilled.

How to Grill a Perfect Steak

Prime or choice sirloin, club, T-bone, and other high-quality steaks don't even need to be marinated. They are flavorful and tender enough to be cooked with no more seasoning than salt and pepper.

For grilled perfection, make sure the meat is allowed to reach room temperature, which usually takes about 30 minutes on the countertop. Wipe the meat dry with paper towels and then season it with salt and pepper. Set the steaks over moderately hot to hot coals about five inches from the heat. Sear the steaks for two or three minutes on each side, turning them with tongs, if possible, to avoid piercing the meat so that none of the precious juices escape. When the steaks are seared on both sides, remove them from the grill, brush the steaks with a little olive oil, and then return the meat to the grill until it reaches the desired degree of doneness. See table on next page.

Total Grilling Times for Perfect Steaks (including searing)

Times may vary depending on the intensity of the coals

steak thickness	rare	medium	medium-well
1 inch	10 minutes	15 minutes	20 minutes
$1^1/_4$ inches to $1^1/_2$ inches	12 minutes	17 minutes	22 minutes
$1^3/_4$ inches to 2 inches	15 minutes	20 minutes	25 minutes

For filet mignon steaks, decrease the cooking times by one minute.

Flip-flop Grilling

When grilling steaks that are thinner than one inch, employ the flip-flop method. Grill the steaks to sear them for two or three minutes over high heat. Then, turn them every minute or so until they are cooked to the desired degree of doneness. Sure, this requires standing at the grill for eight to ten minutes, but it's not hard work and will avoid the disaster of meat that is burned on the outside and undercooked in the center. When steaks and chops are thicker than an inch, such constant flipping is not necessary. Bone-in chicken parts do best when flip-flopped, too.

Grilling Super-thick Steaks

If you are fortunate enough to have a steak that is two and one-half inches thick or thicker, do not cook it directly over hot coals. Grill it using the indirect method, as explained on pages 5–6, and take care that it cooks evenly. If using a gas grill, cook it over low heat. Cover the grill, lifting the cover periodically to check for flare-ups. If the steak is engulfed by flames, move it to a cooler part of the grill and when the flames subside, return the meat to the hotter fire. Remove the grill cover during the last four or five minutes of cooking and move the steak nearer to the heat source so that it will char a little and form a nice crust. Let the meat rest for about five minutes before slicing.

With meat this thick, use a meat thermometer to determine when the meat is done. Very rare beef should be 130°F, and medium-rare beef 140°F. Remove the steak from the grill when the thermometer registers only a few degrees below these temperatures; the meat continues cooking during resting.

Selecting Round Steak

When buying round steak, which is cut from the rump section of the hindquarter, ask the butcher to cut it from the front section of the round. The first few slices of top round are the most tender and flavorful. Top round has very little fat, which is why it so often is marinated to give it flavor and moisture. Round steak makes good London broil, which should be one of the first cuts of the round. It can also be roasted. Its lack of fat means it has little marbling and so while less expensive than other cuts, it is also less flavorful.

Basting with Beer

On a hot summer day, few things taste as good as a cold beer. We also think that beer tastes good on meat. Regardless of what we are grilling—steak, standing rib roast, butterflied leg of lamb, pork loin, chicken, or game—we often baste the grilling meat with dark beer or ale. Brush some beer or ale on the grilling meat two or three times during cooking to give the meat a subtle yet deep flavor. The beer—which does not have to be icy cold, but can be at room temperature—also cools the meat momentarily during grilling, which can help moderate cooking.

What Is Flank Steak?

There is only one flank steak to a side of beef and it comes from the lower section of the short loin. It is a lean, flat, boneless muscle with fibers that run lengthwise through the meat. Flank steak is best when grilled or broiled—it does not lend itself to slow cooking. Once cooked, flank steak should be cut on the diagonal into thin strips, cutting across the fibers. This brings out its flavor and renders the meat tender. Flank steak is the most common cut used in recipes calling for London broil, although in some instances, top round is also called London broil.

The porterhouse is cut from the short loin nearest the sirloin and is popular because of its generous section of tenderloin. It usually is cut to be 1¼ to 3 inches thick. One good-sized steak easily feeds four. Porterhouses are distinguished by their "tail," which should be folded back against the steak and held in place with a small metal or wooden skewer for even grilling. The tail can also be removed, ground, and cooked alongside the steak as a burger. When grilling any steak, but particularly a porterhouse steak with a tail, watch for flare-ups when the fat drips on the coals. Extinguish them with a spritz of water from a spray bottle.

Lobel's Classic Grilled Porterhouse Steak

Serves 4 to 5

3 TO 3½ POUNDS PORTERHOUSE
   STEAK, ABOUT 2 INCHES THICK
METAL OR WOODEN SKEWER
½ LEMON
2 TABLESPOONS OLIVE OIL
2 CLOVES GARLIC, CRUSHED
2 SCALLIONS, WHITE PARTS ONLY,
   FINELY CHOPPED
SALT AND FRESHLY GROUND BLACK
   PEPPER TO TASTE
VEGETABLE OIL COOKING SPRAY

1. Trim the outer fat from the steak (or ask the butcher to do so). Rub the fat with the cut lemon to prevent burning and smoking. Score both sides of the tail of the steak and then fold it back towards the main body and attach it to the meat with a small metal skewer or sturdy wooden skewer. (If using a wooden skewer, soak it in water for about 20 minutes first.)

2. Combine the olive oil, garlic, scallions, salt, and pepper in a glass or ceramic dish. Put the steak in the dish and turn several times to coat. Cover and marinate at room temperature for 1 hour or in the refrigerator for as long as 4 hours. Turn the meat once or twice during marinating.

3. Prepare a charcoal or gas grill. Lightly spray the grill rack with vegetable oil cooking spray. The coals should be moderately hot to hot.

4. Lift the steak from the marinade. Discard the marinade. Grill the steak, covered, for 10 to 12 minutes. Turn and grill, covered, for 10 to 12 minutes longer for medium-rare, or until it reaches the desired degree of doneness. Let the meat rest for a few minutes before serving.

Grill a boneless sirloin or rib steak with this marinade. The weight of the meat is not as important as its thickness, so begin by looking for a nice, thick steak.

Sirloin Steak in Spicy Marinade

Serves 6

3 TO 3½ POUNDS BONELESS SIRLOIN
OR RIB STEAK, ABOUT 2 INCHES
THICK

½ CUP SOY SAUCE

¼ CUP FRESH LEMON JUICE

2 TABLESPOONS OLIVE OIL

2 TEASPOONS GROUND CUMIN

1 TEASPOON CAYENNE PEPPER

2 SCALLIONS, SLICED

1 JALAPEÑO, SEEDED AND SLICED

1 CLOVE GARLIC, MINCED

FRESHLY GROUND BLACK PEPPER TO
TASTE

VEGETABLE OIL COOKING SPRAY

1. Trim the outer fat, or ask the butcher to do so.

2. Combine the soy sauce, lemon juice, oil, cumin, cayenne, scallions, jalapeño, garlic, and pepper in a glass or ceramic bowl. Put the steaks in a glass or ceramic dish and pour the marinade over the meat. Cover and marinate at room temperature for 30 minutes or refrigerate for as long as 2 hours. Turn the meat once or twice.

3. Prepare a charcoal or gas grill. Lightly spray the grill rack with vegetable oil cooking spray. The coals should be moderately hot to hot.

4. Lift the steak from the marinade. Discard the marinade. Grill the steak, covered, for 10 to 12 minutes. Turn and grill, covered, for 10 to 12 minutes longer for medium-rare, or until it reaches desired degree of doneness. Let the meat rest for a few minutes before serving.

The T-bone is easily identified by the T-shaped bone in the center of the cut. The steak comes from the center section of the short loin, between the porterhouse and the club steak—and while it tastes similar to porterhouse, it has a smaller tenderloin and shorter tail. For this recipe, you can substitute porterhouse or club steak.

T-bone for Two

Serves 2 to 3

ONE 2-POUND T-BONE STEAK WITH
  TAIL, ABOUT 2 INCHES THICK
1 TO 2 TABLESPOONS OLIVE OIL
1 TABLESPOON CRACKED BLACK
  PEPPER
1 TEASPOON DRIED ROSEMARY
1 TO 2 TEASPOONS COARSE SALT
VEGETABLE OIL COOKING SPRAY
MUSHROOM-SAGE SAUCE (PAGE 176)

1. Rub the steak with the olive oil, pepper, and rosemary. Set aside for 20 to 30 minutes until ready to grill.

2. Prepare a charcoal or gas grill. Lightly spray the grill rack with vegetable oil cooking spray. The coals should be moderately hot to hot.

3. Rub the salt into both sides of the steak. Grill for 8 to 10 minutes on each side for medium-rare meat. Let the meat rest for a few minutes and serve with the Mushroom-Sage Sauce.

Filet mignon is one of the most popular steaks for grilling. These are also known as tenderloin steaks. The small thick steaks, perfect for individual servings, are soft and tender, which is appealing to grill cooks. But filet mignon is not always as flavorful as other steaks. Therefore, we think it's important to rub it with olive oil, salt, and pepper before grilling to enhance the flavor. Here, we serve each one with a pat of melting flavorful butter, too.

Grilled Filet Mignon with Gorgonzola-Scallion Compound Butter *Serves 4*

4 FILET MIGNONS, EACH 1½ INCHES THICK

1 TO 2 TABLESPOONS OLIVE OIL

1 TABLESPOON CRACKED BLACK PEPPER

VEGETABLE OIL COOKING SPRAY

1 TO 2 TEASPOONS COARSE SALT

4 TABLESPOONS GORGONZOLA-SCALLION COMPOUND BUTTER (PAGE 180) OR HORSERADISH-SCALLION COMPOUND BUTTER (PAGE 179)

1. Rub the steaks with olive oil and pepper. Set aside for 20 to 30 minutes until ready to grill.

2. Prepare a charcoal or gas grill. Lightly spray the grill rack with vegetable oil cooking spray. The coals should be moderately hot to hot.

3. Rub the salt into both sides of the steaks. Grill for 5 to 6 minutes on each side for rare meat or for 6 to 7 minutes for medium-rare meat. Brush a little more olive oil on the steaks after they are turned. Place a pat of butter on top of each filet mignon as soon as it comes off the grill so that the butter begins to melt on top of the meat. Let the meat rest for a few minutes before serving.

For a classic steak au poivre, we recommend as fine a steak as you can find, such as shell steak, also known as New York strip, Kansas City strip, and strip loin. Filet mignon is also good for this recipe.

Grilled Steak au Poivre   *Serves 4*

4 BONELESS SHELL STEAKS, ABOUT 2
   INCHES THICK, EACH WEIGHING 12
   TO 14 OUNCES
¼ CUP CRACKED BLACK OR BLACK AND
   WHITE PEPPERCORNS
VEGETABLE OIL COOKING SPRAY

1. Trim the outer fat from the steak, or ask the butcher to do so.

2. Press the peppercorns into the meat on both sides.

3. Prepare a charcoal or gas grill. Lightly spray the grill rack with vegetable oil cooking spray. The coals should be hot.

4. Grill the steaks for 7 minutes. Turn and grill for 8 to 10 minutes longer for medium-rare, or until they reach desired degree of doneness. Let the meat rest for a few minutes before serving.

Steak holds the claim as the most popular cut of beef, and certainly restaurant chefs would concur. However, there are many different types of steak, so it can be confusing when it comes to grilling. We suggest the higher-end steaks for many of our recipes, such as this one. Flank steaks and round steaks lend themselves to slightly different preparations, and we provide such recipes. Look for the best cut you can find, or ask the butcher for his recommendations. In general, the best steaks for grilling unadorned or in recipes such as this are porterhouse, T-bone, club, sirloin, or shell.

In this recipe, note that the chilies for the sauce can be lightly grilled over the fire before you grill the steak. Be sure to have all the other sauce ingredients ready so that you can prepare the chilies and finish the sauce while the steak grills—or as soon as it is lifted from the grill. If you have a gas grill with a gas burner, use it to cook the sauce.

Grilled Sirloin Steak with Green Chili Sauce   *Serves 6*

STEAK

3³/₄ TO 4-POUNDS BONELESS SIRLOIN,
   ABOUT 2 INCHES THICK
1 TABLESPOON OLIVE OIL
¹/₂ TEASPOON CRUSHED CUMIN SEED
1 TEASPOON DRIED OREGANO
1 TEASPOON DRIED THYME LEAVES
1 CLOVE GARLIC
SALT AND FRESHLY GROUND BLACK
   PEPPER TO TASTE
VEGETABLE OIL COOKING SPRAY

1. To prepare the steak, trim the outer fat from the steak, or ask the butcher to do so.

2. Rub the entire surface of the meat with the olive oil. Combine the cumin, oregano, thyme, garlic, salt, and pepper in a small bowl. Using your fingers, rub evenly on both sides of the steak and put the steak in a shallow glass or ceramic dish. Cover and refrigerate for at least 1 hour or overnight.

3. To prepare the sauce, prepare a charcoal or gas grill or pre-heat the broiler. If using a grill, the coals should be moderately hot. Set the chilies over the heat or under the broiler and grill or broil for about 5 minutes on each side until lightly charred and fragrant. Remove from the grill or broiler and set aside in a paper bag or cover with a thickness of paper towels to cool. When cool enough to handle, peel the skin using your fingers or a dull knife. (Do not peel the

SAUCE

6 FRESH ANAHEIM GREEN CHILIES

1 TABLESPOON CANOLA OIL

1 ONION, HALVED, AND THINLY SLICED
   CROSSWISE

1 LARGE CLOVE GARLIC, SLICED

1 CUP HALF-AND-HALF

3 TABLESPOONS CREAM CHEESE

3 TABLESPOONS SOUR CREAM

SALT TO TASTE

chilies under running water or their flavor will be diluted.) Cut off and discard the stems and caps. Slit the chilies, scrape out the seeds (don't worry if a few remain), and slice the chilies. You will have about 1 cup of chilies.

4. Meanwhile, prepare a charcoal or gas grill. Lightly spray the grill rack with vegetable oil cooking spray. The coals should be moderately hot to hot.

5. Heat the oil in a skillet over medium heat. Add the onions and garlic and cook, stirring, for about 5 minutes, or until the onions are softened. Add the chilies and cook for 3 to 4 minutes longer, or until fragrant.

6. Increase the heat to medium-high and add the half-and-half. Cook, stirring, for about 10 minutes, or until the sauce is reduced by half. Cover and set aside to keep warm while grilling the steak.

7. Grill the steak for 10 to 12 minutes. Turn and grill for 10 to 12 minutes longer for medium-rare, or until it reaches desired degree of doneness. Let the meat rest for a few minutes before serving.

8. Set the pan with the chili sauce over low heat. Add the cream cheese and stir until smooth. Stir in the sour cream and season with salt. While stirring, heat the sauce just until hot. Do not let the sauce boil. Serve immediately with the steak.

Any tender steak tastes great with classic teriyaki marinade. In this recipe we suggest porterhouse, but you won't go wrong with sirloin or T-bone. The T-bone comes from the center section of the short loin, between the porterhouse and the club steak, and, although it has a smaller fillet, is very similar in texture and flavor to the porterhouse. If you would rather grill these fine steaks without marinating them first, please do. Use the marinade, too, on round steak or rib steak. Rib steaks are less tender and fattier than club steaks, which they resemble in appearance. Round steaks are from the rump and are quite lean, which is why they do well when marinated—the lack of fat means the meat is drier than other cuts and so benefits from a good soaking in a flavorful liquid.

Teriyaki Steak with Grilled Pineapple
Serves 6

3³/₄ TO 4 POUNDS PORTERHOUSE STEAKS, ABOUT 2 INCHES THICK
METAL OR WOODEN SKEWER
1 CUP TERIYAKI MARINADE (PAGE 191)
VEGETABLE OIL COOKING SPRAY
SIX 1¹/₂- TO 2-INCH-THICK FRESH OR CANNED AND DRAINED PINEAPPLE RINGS
CANOLA OIL
¹/₄ CUP BROWN SUGAR

1. Trim the outer fat from the steaks, or ask the butcher to do so. Score both sides of the tail of the steak and then fold it back towards the main body and attach it to the meat with a small metal skewer or sturdy wooden skewer. (If using a wooden skewer, soak it in water for about 20 minute first.)

2. Put the steaks in a shallow glass or ceramic dish and pour the marinade over the meat, turning several times to coat. Cover and marinate at room temperature for 30 minutes or refrigerate for as long as 2 hours. Turn the meat once or twice.

3. Prepare a charcoal or gas grill. Lightly spray the grill rack with vegetable oil cooking spray. The coals should be moderately hot to hot.

4. Lift the steaks from the marinade. Discard the marinade. Grill the steaks for 10 to 12 minutes. Turn and grill for 10 to 12 minutes longer for medium-rare, or until it reaches the desired degree of doneness. Let the meat rest for a few minutes before serving.

5. Meanwhile, brush the pineapple slices on both sides with a little canola oil and sprinkle each one with about 2 teaspoons of brown sugar. Lay sugared side down on the outer edge of the grill, away from the hottest heat. Grill for about 7 minutes, turn, and grill for 6 or 7 minutes longer, or until lightly browned and tender. Serve set on top or alongside the steak.

Hanger steak is also known as "butcher's tenderloin" because traditionally butchers saved this full-flavored but unattractive-looking cut for themselves. It "hangs" between the rib cage and the loin cage, which explains its name. All hanger steaks are approximately the same size and weight. In recent years, it has become popular with chefs and steak lovers, and once you try one, you will understand why. Hanger steak needs no fancy preparation, just a brushing of oil and a little salt and pepper. You probably will not find hanger steaks in the meat section of the supermarket, but ask a good butcher for one, making sure it is prime or choice beef. Hanger steak also makes great hamburgers. It's best to remove the center vein, which runs lengthwise down the center of the steak. This leaves the steak in two pieces, neither of uniform thickness, which can make uniform grilling tricky—but well worth the effort.

Grilled Hanger Steak   *Serves 2 to 3*

VEGETABLE OIL COOKING SPRAY

1 HANGER STEAK, TRIMMED AND
    CENTER VEIN REMOVED

OLIVE OIL

COARSE OR KOSHER SALT AND FRESHLY
    GROUND BLACK PEPPER TO TASTE

1. Prepare a charcoal or gas grill. Lightly spray the grill rack with vegetable oil cooking spray. The coals should be moderately hot to hot.

2. Brush the steak with olive oil and sprinkle on both sides with salt and pepper. Gently press the salt and pepper into the meat.

3. Sear the meat for about 1 minute on each side and then grill for 12 to 15 minutes, depending on the thickness of the steak. If the thin end of the steak cooks before the fatter end is done, position the steak so that the thin end is on the edge of the grill. Turn the steak frequently during grilling. Let it rest for about 5 minutes before slicing.

We suggest top round for this steak salad, since it is tender enough and is a perfect steak for marinating. However, you can use a more expensive cut, too, such as shell, which is also called New York strip, Kansas City strip, or plain strip. Or use sirloin tip, which is boneless sirloin and is the bottom tip of the sirloin section. Sirloin tip is not quite as tender as other sirloin cuts but it has great flavor. For grilling, use sturdy straight scallions—not any that are too slender or too bulbous.

Grilled Steak Salad with Grilled Mushrooms and Scallions   *Serves 6*

STEAK AND VEGETABLES

2¹/₂ POUNDS TOP ROUND STEAK,
 ABOUT 1¹/₂ INCH THICK, TRIMMED

1 RECIPE RED WINE VINEGAR
 MARINADE (PAGE 188)

VEGETABLE OIL COOKING SPRAY

2 LARGE PORTOBELLO MUSHROOMS
 (ABOUT ¹/₂ POUND), STEMMED

3 TO 4 SCALLIONS, TRIMMED

2 TO 3 TABLESPOONS OLIVE OIL

VINAIGRETTE

¹/₄ CUP BALSAMIC VINEGAR

2 TEASPOONS DIJON MUSTARD

¹/₂ CUP OLIVE OIL

SALT AND FRESHLY GROUND BLACK
 PEPPER TO TASTE

1. Put the steak in a glass or ceramic dish and add the marinade, turning the steak several times to coat. Cover and refrigerate for 2 to 4 hours.

2. Prepare a charcoal or gas grill. Lightly spray the grill rack with vegetable oil cooking spray. The coals should be moderately hot to hot.

3. Lift the steak from the marinade, letting most of the marinade drip back into the dish. Grill the meat for 8 to 10 minutes, brushing several times with the marinade during the first 5 minutes of grilling. (The oil in the marinade may cause flare-ups.) Turn and grill for 8 to 10 minutes longer until medium-rare, or until it reaches the desired degree of doneness. Let cool.

4. While the steak grills, lay the mushrooms and scallions near the outside of the grill away from the most intense heat, brush with oil, and grill for 8 to 10 minutes, turning once or twice and brushing with more oil, until the mushrooms are tender and the scallions are lightly browned and tender.

SALAD

1 HEAD BOSTON OR RED LEAF LETTUCE

1 BUNCH ARUGULA

2 RIPE TOMATOES, SLICED

½ CUP NIÇOISE OR KALAMATA OLIVES

½ CUP CRUMBLED FETA CHEESE
   (ABOUT 2 OUNCES)

5. Slice the steak and mushrooms into strips and transfer to a bowl. Cut the scallions into short lengths and transfer to the bowl.

6. To make the vinaigrette, whisk together the vinegar and mustard. Still whisking, slowly add the oil, whisking until emulsified. Season with salt and pepper. Pour half the vinaigrette over the warm steak and vegetables and toss gently to coat. Set aside for about 30 minutes to cool to room temperature. (If setting aside for any longer, cover, and refrigerate; bring to room temperature before serving.)

7. Arrange the lettuce and arugula on a platter. Spoon the meat and vegetables over the lettuce. Garnish with the tomatoes and olives and sprinkle with the cheese. Pass the remaining vinaigrette on the side, whisking well before serving.

For these kabobs, use boned sirloin or any other tender steak, such as shell steak or sirloin tip. Filet mignon or filet mignon tips would work well, too, particularly since this recipe does not call for lengthy marinating, which would be a waste with really good meat. Use thin-skinned potatoes and brush them gently when cleaning to avoid tearing the skins.

Sirloin Steak Kabobs with Rosemary-Brushed Potatoes and Red Peppers
Serves 6

6 SMALL RED-SKINNED POTATOES
(ABOUT 1 POUND)

SALT TO TASTE

1/2 CUP OLIVE OIL

2 CLOVES GARLIC, CRUSHED

3 TABLESPOONS CHOPPED FRESH
ROSEMARY

FRESHLY GROUND BLACK PEPPER TO
TASTE

VEGETABLE OIL COOKING SPRAY

2 1/2 POUNDS SIRLOIN STEAK, TRIMMED
AND CUT INTO 24 CUBES, EACH
ABOUT 1 1/2 INCHES SQUARE

3 RED BELL PEPPERS (ABOUT 1 1/2
POUNDS), CUT INTO 18 CHUNKS

SIX 12-INCH METAL SKEWERS

1. Put the potatoes in a large saucepan and add enough water to cover by 2 or 3 inches. Lightly salt the water and bring to a boil over high heat. Reduce the heat and simmer briskly for about 15 minutes until the potatoes are just fork-tender. Drain and cool to room temperature. Cut into halves so that there are 12 pieces. Handle the potatoes gently to prevent the skin from slipping off.

2. Combine the olive oil, garlic, and rosemary in a large bowl; season to taste with salt and pepper. Add the potatoes and stir gently to coat.

3. Prepare a charcoal or gas grill. Lightly spray the grill rack with vegetable oil cooking spray. The coals should be moderately hot to hot.

4. Lift the potatoes from the marinade. Transfer the marinade to a small saucepan and heat gently until warm and fragrant. Thread the potatoes, steak, and peppers onto skewers, beginning and ending with a potato and threading 4 pieces of meat and 3 chunks of peppers onto each. Grill for 10 to 12 minutes, turning several times and brushing with the warm marinade, until medium-rare, or until the meat reaches the desired degree of doneness, the potatoes are tender, and the peppers are slightly charred. Serve immediately.

From the rump—also called round, skirt, or flank of the steer—round steak may be sold with a small, round bone or not, depending on the butcher. It is lean and not as juicy as some other steaks, which is one reason it lends itself so well to marinating, slicing thin after grilling, and then serving with other flavorful ingredients, such as tomatoes, jalapeños, and salsa.

Tortilla-Wrapped Round Steak   *Serves 6*

1½ POUNDS ROUND STEAK, TRIMMED, ABOUT 1½ INCHES THICK

1 RECIPE TOASTED CUMIN MARINADE (PAGE 190)

VEGETABLE OIL COOKING SPRAY

1 LARGE WHITE ONION, CUT ABOUT ½ INCH THICK

2 TO 3 TABLESPOONS CANOLA OIL

COARSELY GROUND BLACK PEPPER TO TASTE

TWELVE 7-INCH FLOUR TORTILLAS

CHOPPED TOMATOES

CHOPPED PICKLED JALAPEÑO PEPPERS

CHOPPED CILANTRO OR FLAT-LEAF PARSLEY

BAJA-STYLE TOMATO SALSA (PAGE 185) (OPTIONAL)

1. Put the steak in a glass or ceramic dish and add the marinade, turning the steaks several times to coat. Cover and refrigerate for 4 to 8 hours.

2. Prepare a charcoal or gas grill. Lightly spray the grill rack with vegetable oil cooking spray. The coals should be moderately hot to hot.

3. Lift the steak from the marinade, letting the marinade drip back into the dish. Grill the meat for 8 minutes, brushing several times with the marinade during the first 5 minutes of grilling. (The oil in the marinade may cause flare-ups.) Turn and grill for 8 to 10 minutes longer until medium-rare, or until it reaches desired degree of doneness. Let the meat rest for a few minutes.

4. Place the onion slices near the outside of the grill away from the most intense heat, brush with oil, and sprinkle with the pepper. Turn once or twice, brushing with more oil, and grill for 8 to 10 minutes, or until the onions are lightly browned and tender. While they cook, wrap the tortillas in foil, place the packet on the outside edge of the grill, and let the tortillas warm while the steak and onions are cooking.

5. Slice the steak into strips and separate the onions into rings. Arrange the steak, onions, chopped tomatoes, and jalapeños in the tortillas and wrap into a sandwich. Garnish with cilantro and top with salsa, if desired.

Rib roast, also called prime rib, is from the rib section of the forequarter and is a favorite for celebrations and holidays. The ribs encase wonderfully tender, juicy, and flavorful meat that is perfectly marbled and covered with a substantial layer of fat. Large rib roasts include the short ribs and can serve up to 16 people. Smaller ones, such as we suggest for grilling, are trimmed, with the short ribs removed, and are great for four to six people. For the grill, buy a three- or four-rib roast. All the roast needs is a little sliced garlic and salt and pepper. It has enough fat and so requires no olive oil. You will love how a rib roast tastes when grilled, served with the Horseradish Cream Sauce on page 175. When we grill a standing rib roast, we sometimes like to baste it with dark beer to deepen its flavor.

Grilled Standing Rib Roast   *Serves 4 to 6*

VEGETABLE OIL COOKING SPRAY

ONE 3½- TO 4-POUND STANDING RIB
    ROAST (3 RIBS)

1 LARGE CLOVE GARLIC, THINLY CUT
    INTO WIDE SLICES

COARSE SALT AND FRESHLY GROUND
    BLACK PEPPER TO TASTE

HORSERADISH CREAM SAUCE

1. Prepare a charcoal or gas grill, arranging the coals for indirect cooking. Lightly spray the grill rack with vegetable oil cooking spray. The coals should be moderately hot to hot.

2. Using a sharp knife, make small slits down the meaty side of the roast. Insert the garlic in the slits. Sprinkle with salt and pepper.

3. Sear the meat over intense heat on the bone side and the narrow sides for 1 or 2 minutes per side. Sear the meaty side (top) for about 3 minutes. Turn the roast with tongs, if possible, to avoid piercing the meat so that none of the juices escape.

4. Transfer the roast, bone side down, to the cooler part of the grill. Cover the grill and cook for 1 hour and 20 minutes to 1 hour and 30 minutes for rare, or longer for more well-done meat. After 1 hour, insert an instant-read meat thermometer into the thickest part of the meat (not too close to a bone). When the thermometer registers 130° (for rare meat) to 140°F (for medium-rare meat), remove the roast from the grill and let rest for 5 to 10 minutes before carving. Do not overcook. Serve with the Horseradish Cream Sauce.

Flank steak is lean, flat, boneless meat. Because its fibers run lengthwise, it is best to slice it on an angle, which means perpendicular to the long, fine fibers running through the meat. For six servings, you may have to buy it in two smaller pieces to equal three pounds.

Thai-Style Marinated Flank Steak   *Serves 6*

¼ CUP RICE WINE VINEGAR

¼ CUP FRESH LIME JUICE

¼ CUP DARK, TOASTED SESAME OIL

¼ CUP SOY SAUCE

ASIAN CHILI SAUCE, TO TASTE (SEE NOTE)

2 TABLESPOONS CHOPPED FRESH GINGER

2 TABLESPOONS CHOPPED SCALLIONS

2 TO 3 CLOVES GARLIC, CHOPPED

2 TO 3 TABLESPOONS CHOPPED CILANTRO PLUS CHOPPED CILANTRO FOR GARNISH

SALT AND FRESHLY GROUND BLACK PEPPER TO TASTE

3 POUNDS 1¼-INCH-THICK FLANK STEAK OR LONDON BROIL, TRIMMED

VEGETABLE OIL COOKING SPRAY

1. Whisk together all the ingredients, except the steak and cilantro used for garnish, in a shallow glass or ceramic dish. Put the steak in the marinade, turning several times to coat. Cover and refrigerate for at least 1 hour and as long as 8 hours.

2. Prepare a charcoal or gas grill. Lightly spray the grill rack with vegetable oil cooking spray. The coals should be moderately hot to hot.

3. Lift the steak from the marinade, letting the marinade drip back into the dish. Grill the meat for 6 or 7 minutes, brushing several times with the marinade during the first 5 minutes of grilling. (The oil in the marinade may cause flare-ups.) Turn the steak and grill for 6 to 7 minutes longer until medium-rare, or until it reaches the desired degree of doneness.

4. Let the steak rest at room temperature for about 5 minutes before slicing on the diagonal into thin strips. Serve garnished with cilantro.

note: Asian chili sauce is sold in most supermarkets and Asian markets. It may be Chinese-, Thai-, or Vietnamese-style and will vary in heat and intensity. It usually is made from red chilies, but some are made from green chilies. The kind you use does not matter as much as your own preference.

As with the preceding recipe, you may need to buy two pieces of meat for three pounds of flank steak. London broil and flank steak are practically synonymous—although some London broils are cut from the top round.

Thyme-Mustard Crusted Flank Steak   *Serves 6*

3 TABLESPOONS DIJON MUSTARD

1 TABLESPOON WHITE WINE

1 TABLESPOON CHOPPED FRESH THYME

   OR 1 TEASPOON DRIED

1 TABLESPOON CRACKED PEPPER

2 TABLESPOONS OLIVE OIL

3 POUNDS 1½-INCH-THICK FLANK

   STEAK OR LONDON BROIL, TRIMMED

VEGETABLE OIL COOKING SPRAY

1. Stir together the mustard, wine, thyme, and pepper in a small bowl. Whisk in the olive oil.

2. Place the steak in a single layer in a shallow ceramic or glass dish. Spoon the mustard mixture over the meat, spreading to cover. Turn the meat and coat the other side. Cover and refrigerate for at least 2 hours or set aside at room temperature for no longer than 30 minutes.

3. Prepare a charcoal or gas grill. Lightly spray the grill rack with vegetable oil cooking spray. The coals should be moderately hot to hot.

4. Lift the steak from the marinade. Grill the meat for 6 or 7 minutes, brushing several times with the marinade during the first 5 minutes of grilling. (The oil in the marinade may cause flare-ups.) Close the lid on the grill and cook for 2 to 3 minutes longer, or until the mustard coating turns crispy. Turn the steak, cover, and grill for 6 to 7 minutes longer until medium-rare, or until it reaches desired doneness.

5. Let the steak rest at room temperature for about 5 minutes before slicing on the diagonal into thin strips.

London broil is usually flank steak, although the term is used for any thin cut of meat that is broiled or grilled and sliced on the diagonal, or bias. Be sure always to slice London broil into thin strips and on an angle to cut through the lengthwise fibers. For six servings, you may have to buy two pieces of meat for three-and-a-half pounds.

Bloody Mary London Broil   *Serves 6*

2 CUPS TOMATO JUICE

¼ CUP WORCESTERSHIRE SAUCE

3 TABLESPOONS PREPARED COMMER-
   CIAL HORSERADISH

3 TABLESPOONS DRY SHERRY

2 TEASPOONS CRUMBLED DRIED
   MARJORAM

1 TEASPOON CRUMBLED DRIED BASIL

1 TEASPOON FRESHLY GROUND BLACK
   PEPPER

3½ POUNDS LONDON BROIL, ABOUT
   1½ INCHES THICK, TRIMMED

VEGETABLE OIL COOKING SPRAY

1. Stir together the tomato juice, Worcestershire sauce, horse-radish, sherry, marjoram, basil, and pepper in a small bowl.

2. Place the steak in a single layer in a glass or ceramic dish. Spoon the tomato-juice mixture over the meat, spreading to cover. Turn the meat to coat the other side. Cover and refrigerate for at least 2 hours or set aside at room temperature for no longer than 30 minutes.

3. Prepare a charcoal or gas grill. Lightly spray the grill rack with vegetable oil cooking spray. The coals should be moderately hot to hot.

4. Lift the meat from the marinade. Discard the marinade. Grill the steak for 8 minutes. Turn the steak and grill for 7 to 10 minutes longer for medium-rare, or until it reaches the desired doneness.

5. Let the steak rest at room temperature for about 5 minutes before slicing on the diagonal into thin strips.

Beef chuck, cut from the forequarter, is juicy and flavorful. It has some fat and so is a good choice for slow, moist cooking such as a stew or pot roast. Chuck often is sold on the bone, but it is also available boneless. Rump roast or top or bottom round could also be used for this stew, although they are not quite as fatty and so may be a little dry. Cooking stew on the grill is easy, requiring practically no tending once the ingredients are mixed together. We highly recommend having the vegetables and other ingredients prepped and ready to go before you start cooking. This will make the process effortless, and the result is a rich, full-bodied stew with tender meat and vegetables infused with a very slight smokiness that can only be achieved on a grill. This is one of our favorites. For the most intense charcoal-grilled flavor, cook this on a charcoal fire rather than a gas grill—although it is delicious either way.

Grilled Beef Stew   *Serves 6 to 8*

2¹/₂ TO 2³/₄ POUNDS BONELESS BEEF
   CHUCK, CUT INTO 1 TO 1¹/₂ INCH
   CUBES

¹/₂ CUP ALL-PURPOSE FLOUR

1 TEASPOON PAPRIKA

2 CUPS BEEF BROTH

1 CUP DRY RED WINE

1 TABLESPOON TOMATO PASTE

2 LARGE BAY LEAVES

4 SPRIGS FRESH THYME

2 TEASPOONS SALT

1 TEASPOON FRESHLY GROUND BLACK
   PEPPER

4 OUNCES BACON, DICED

1 POUND FRESH PEARL ONIONS,
   PEELED (SEE NOTE)

1.   Prepare a charcoal or gas grill. The coals should be moderately hot.

2.   Toss the beef cubes with the flour and paprika in a shallow dish. Discard any excess flour and set the meat aside.

3.   Stir the broth, wine, tomato paste, bay leaves, thyme, salt, and pepper together in a large bowl.

4.   Put a foil roasting pan, about 12 × 18 inches large, on the grill. Cook the bacon in the pan for 3 to 5 minutes, stirring, until the fat is rendered but the bacon is not browned. Add the onions and garlic cloves, cover the grill, and cook for about 5 minutes, shaking the pan and stirring several times. Add the mushrooms, cover the grill, and cook for about 5 minutes. Using a slotted spoon, spoon the contents of the pan into a large bowl, add the potatoes and carrots, and toss to mix. Set aside.

6 CLOVES GARLIC, PEELED

1 POUND BABY WHITE MUSHROOMS
(SEE NOTE)

1 POUND THIN-SKINNED RED POTA-
TOES, CUT INTO 1-INCH CUBES

1 POUND CARROTS, CUT INTO 1-INCH
CUBES

5. Put the meat in the roasting pan, stirring to coat it with the pan juices. Spread the meat in a single layer, cover the grill, and cook for about 10 minutes, stirring several times to brown on all sides. Remove the roasting pan from the heat.

6. Pour the wine mixture into the pan and add the vegetables. Stir to mix, shaking the pan to distribute the food evenly. Wrap 2 large sheets of heavy-duty foil around the pan, completely encasing it for a sealed package. Return the pan to the grill.

7. Cover the grill and let the stew cook for about 1 hour. Add fresh coals to the grill as needed to maintain a moderately hot temperature. Shake the pan every 8 to 10 minutes to ensure even cooking. Do not unwrap the pan for at least 1 hour during cooking. Unwrap the stew and check for doneness. The stew is done when the meat is cooked through and the potatoes and carrots are tender.

note: Pearl onions are the size of marbles. If you cannot find fresh pearl onions, substitute plain, frozen pearl onions—not the brine-packed canned onions. You could also cut a large onion into small wedges. Use baby mushrooms or cut larger white mushrooms into halves or quarters. The important thing is to have vegetables of uniform size.

To enhance the char-cooked flavor of the meat, thread the uncooked meat onto metal skewers, brush with a little oil, and grill over a moderately hot fire for 10 to 15 minutes, turning several times until browned. This replaces step 5 above, in which the meat is browned in the pan.

Brisket is the fatty, fibrous cut of meat behind the foreshank and below the chuck. The second cut of the brisket, toward the shoulder, is the cut most often preferred for corned beef and for grilling. Note that when grilling brisket, it has to be precooked for several hours before it is grilled. Here, we parboil it and when it is tender, rub it with a dry rub, allow it to marinate in its own juices, and then finish it on the grill.

Grilled Peppery Beef Brisket   *Serves 6 to 8*

6 POUNDS BEEF BRISKET, TRIMMED

1 LARGE ONION, COARSELY CHOPPED
   OR SLICED

3 CLOVES GARLIC, CRUSHED

5 OR 6 PEPPERCORNS

1/4 CUP PEPPERY DRY RUB (PAGE 193)

VEGETABLE OIL COOKING SPRAY

MADISON AVENUE BARBECUE SAUCE
   (PAGE 173)

1. Combine the brisket, onion, garlic, and peppercorns in a stockpot or large saucepan. Add enough water to cover the meat by about 1 inch. Bring to a boil over high heat, reduce the heat to medium-low, and cook, covered, for 2 to 2$\frac{1}{2}$ hours, or until the meat is tender when pierced with a fork. Check the meat for tenderness after 2 hours.

2. Lift the meat from the cooking liquid and discard the liquid. When the meat is cool enough to handle, pat dry with paper towels. Rub all sides of the brisket with the dry rub, transfer to a shallow dish, cover loosely, and set aside at room temperature for about 1 hour, or refrigerate for as long as 24 hours. Alternatively, put the brisket in a sealable plastic bag and refrigerate.

3. Prepare a charcoal or gas grill. Lightly spray the grill rack with vegetable oil cooking spray. The coals should be moderately hot.

4. Grill the brisket for about 20 minutes. Turn and cook for 20 minutes longer, or until the internal temperature is between 190° and 200°F. Let the meat rest for about 15 minutes before slicing thinly across the grain. Serve with the barbecue sauce.

Brisket needs precooking before grilling. In this recipe, it is baked after first marinating in a dry rub. Following a stint on the grill, we serve it with the same barbecue sauce that flavors it during baking. For a smoky flavor, toss some soaked wood chips on the fire during grilling (see page 4).

Sweet 'n Spicy Barbecued Brisket

Serves 6 to 8

6 POUNDS BEEF BRISKET, TRIMMED

SWEET 'N SPICY DRY RUB (PAGE 195)

2 TABLESPOONS CANOLA OIL

1/2 CUP FINELY CHOPPED ONIONS

1 CLOVE GARLIC, FINELY CHOPPED

1 TEASPOON CRUSHED RED PEPPER

1 TEASPOON DRIED MARJORAM

1 TEASPOON DRY MUSTARD

3 CUPS TOMATO PUREE

1/2 CUP ORANGE JUICE

1/2 CUP CIDER VINEGAR

1/4 CUP FIRMLY PACKED LIGHT OR DARK
    BROWN SUGAR

1 TEASPOON SALT

VEGETABLE OIL COOKING SPRAY

1. Rub all sides of the brisket with the dry rub, transfer it to a shallow dish, and cover loosely. Set aside at room temperature for about 1 hour, or refrigerate for as long as 24 hours. Alternatively, put the brisket in a sealable plastic bag and refrigerate.

2. Heat the oil in a saucepan over medium heat. Add the onions and garlic and cook, stirring, for about 10 minutes, or until the onions soften and are translucent. Add the crushed red pepper, marjoram, and mustard and cook, stirring, for 1 minute. Add the tomato puree, orange juice, vinegar, sugar, and salt and bring to a simmer, stirring to dissolve the sugar. Reduce the heat and simmer gently for about 30 minutes, or until slightly thickened.

3. Preheat the oven to 325°F.

4. Spread a thin layer of the sauce over the bottom of a roasting pan just large enough to hold the brisket. Put the brisket in the pan and spread a little more sauce over it. Cover the pan tightly with foil and bake for about 2 hours, or until tender.

5. Prepare a charcoal or gas grill. Lightly spray the grill rack with vegetable oil cooking spray. The coals should be moderately hot.

6. Grill the brisket for about 20 minutes. Turn and cook for 20 minutes longer, or until the internal temperature is between 190° and 200°F. Let the meat rest for about 15 minutes before slicing thinly across the grain.

7. Reheat the sauce over medium heat. Serve with the brisket.

Corned beef is brisket that has been cured in brine. Old-fashioned corned beef was quite salty, but nowadays the brine is less salty and usually contains no nitrites. Like brisket, corned beef must be parboiled for hours before it can be prepared for grilling. During grilling, watch for flare-ups, since the corned beef is fatty. Move the meat to a cooler part of the grill until the flames subside or while dousing them with water. When you buy corned beef, it comes packed in Cryovac with explicit cooking instructions. Follow them or follow ours; they are similar.

Grilled Glazed Corned Beef *Serves 6*

ONE 4- TO 4½-POUND CORNED BEEF
  BRISKET, TRIMMED
1 TABLESPOON CANOLA OIL
1 TABLESPOON FROZEN ORANGE JUICE
  CONCENTRATE
1 TABLESPOON ORANGE-FLAVORED
  LIQUEUR, SUCH AS COINTREAU OR
  GRAND MARNIER
1 CLOVE GARLIC, FINELY CHOPPED
1½ TEASPOONS DARK BROWN SUGAR
½ TEASPOON GROUND GINGER
½ TEASPOON CHOPPED FRESH GINGER
½ TEASPOON GROUND CINNAMON
¼ TEASPOON DRY MUSTARD
VEGETABLE OIL COOKING SPRAY

1. Cook the corned beef according to the package instructions or by following this method: Combine the corned beef brisket and enough water to cover by 2 or 3 inches in a large stockpot. Add the spice pouch included with the beef (if the corned beef you buy does not have a spice pouch, add 2 or 3 black peppercorns to the water). Bring to a boil over high heat. Reduce the heat and simmer for 2½ to 3 hours, or until the beef is tender when pierced with a fork. Lift the corned beef from the water, cool slightly, and pat dry.

2. Combine the remaining ingredients in a small bowl and stir well.

3. Put the corned beef in a glass or ceramic dish and spoon the orange-brown sugar mixture over the meat, rubbing it into the beef on both sides. Cover and refrigerate for at least 4 hours or overnight. Alternatively, rub the mixture into the meat, put the meat in a sealable plastic bag, and refrigerate.

4. Prepare a charcoal or gas grill, arranging the coals for indirect cooking. Lightly spray the grill rack with vegetable oil cooking spray. The coals should be hot.

5. Place the corned beef, fat side down, over the hottest part of the fire and sear for about 10 minutes to make defined grill marks. Transfer to the cooler part of the grill, fat side down, cover, and grill for 20 minutes. Turn the beef and grill for about 10 minutes, or until heated through and nicely browned and crusty.

These ribs are parboiled before being finished on the grill. This is a time-honored way of "grilling" short ribs, which are typically braised when cooked indoors. Meaty ribs are the best bet for grilling; ask the butcher to cut them into manageable lengths, if necessary.

Garlicky Grilled Short Ribs   *Serves 6*

6 TO 8 POUNDS MEATY SHORT RIBS,
   CUT INTO 4- TO 5½-INCH-LONG
   RIBS, TRIMMED

2 TEASPOONS SALT

1 CUP CANOLA OIL

1 CUP TOMATO PASTE

1 CUP DRY SHERRY

3 TABLESPOONS MINCED ONION

8 LARGE CLOVES GARLIC, MINCED

1½ CUPS LIGHTLY PACKED LIGHT OR
   DARK BROWN SUGAR

2 TABLESPOONS WORCESTERSHIRE
   SAUCE

1½ TABLESPOONS HONEY

VEGETABLE OIL COOKING SPRAY

1. Put the ribs in a large stockpot. Add cold water to cover and the salt and bring to a boil over high heat. Reduce the heat to medium-low, skim the foam, cover partially, and simmer for about 1½ hours, or until fork tender. Drain and set aside until cool enough to handle.

2. Combine the oil, tomato paste, sherry, onion, garlic, brown sugar, Worcestershire sauce, and honey in a glass or ceramic bowl and whisk until mixed. Rub the mixture into the meat, cover, and set aside for no longer than 45 minutes at room temperature or for as long as 4 hours refrigerated.

3. Prepare a charcoal or gas grill. Lightly spray the grill rack with vegetable oil cooking spray. The coals should be moderately hot to hot.

4. Lift the ribs from the marinade. Transfer the marinade to a saucepan and cook over medium-high heat until boiling. Reduce the heat to medium and simmer briskly for 5 minutes. Cover and keep warm.

5. Put the ribs on the grill, meat side down, cover, and grill for about 10 minutes. Turn and grill for 8 to 10 minutes longer, or until nicely browned. Cut between the ribs and serve with the marinade.

Also known as flanken, short ribs are cut from the ends of the rib roast and the plate and are composed of layers of lean meat and fat with flat rib bones in between. They are one of the surprises of the grill—tasty and meaty and downright delicious when properly seasoned and cooked. We offer two different methods for grilling short ribs and invite you to try both before settling on one that suits you: They can be parboiled or, as here, baked and then held in the refrigerator until ready to grill. This makes planning easy.

Short Ribs with Quick Barbecue Sauce *Serves 6 to 8*

3 TABLESPOONS OLIVE OIL

3 TABLESPOONS CIDER VINEGAR

1 1/2 TABLESPOONS DRIED OREGANO

1 TABLESPOON SWEET PAPRIKA

1 TABLESPOON FRESHLY GROUND
BLACK PEPPER

1 1/2 TEASPOONS SALT

6 TO 8 POUNDS MEATY SHORT RIBS,
CUT INTO 4- TO 5 1/2-INCH LONG
RIBS, TRIMMED

VEGETABLE OIL COOKING SPRAY

QUICK BARBECUE SAUCE (PAGE 174)

1. Combine the oil, vinegar, oregano, paprika, pepper, and salt in a small bowl and mix well. Rub the paste over the ribs, working it into the meat. Cover and refrigerate for at least 3 hours or overnight. Alternatively, put the ribs in a sealable plastic bag and refrigerate.

2. Preheat the oven to 300°F. Lightly spray a roasting pan large enough to hold the ribs snugly with vegetable oil cooking spray.

3. Place the ribs in the pan in a single layer and cover the pan tightly with foil. Bake for 1 1/2 to 2 hours, or until the meat is tender enough to pierce easily with a knife.

4. Prepare a charcoal or gas grill. Lightly spray the grill rack with vegetable oil cooking spray. The coals should be moderately hot to hot.

5. Heat the sauce in a small pan over medium heat. Brush the ribs generously with the sauce.

6. Put the ribs on the grill, meat side down, cover, and grill for about 10 minutes. Turn and grill for 8 to 10 minutes longer, or until nicely browned. Cut between the ribs and serve with the sauce.

Cooking meat loaf over hot coals gives it wonderful flavor and juicy tenderness. Though it is encased in foil, the meat develops a pleasing crust. We combine three kinds of ground meat for flavor and moisture. You may substitute all beef, but if so, combine ground sirloin with chuck for the fat content and resulting moisture. This recipe makes a hefty meatloaf, but the left-overs are out of this world.

Grilled Meat Loaf   *Serves 6 to 8*

VEGETABLE OIL COOKING SPRAY

1½ CUPS SEASONED DRIED ITALIAN-
STYLE BREAD CRUMBS

2 TABLESPOONS GRATED ONION

2 CLOVES GARLIC, MINCED

½ TEASPOON SALT

½ TEASPOON CRUSHED DRIED
OREGANO

½ TEASPOON CRUSHED DRIED THYME

¼ TEASPOON FRESHLY GROUND BLACK
PEPPER

½ CUP HALF-AND-HALF

1 POUND GROUND BEEF SIRLOIN

1 POUND GROUND VEAL

1 POUND GROUND PORK

1. Prepare a charcoal or gas grill. Lightly spray the grill rack with vegetable oil cooking spray. The coals should be moderately hot.

2. Combine the bread crumbs, onions, garlic, salt, oregano, thyme, pepper, and half-and-half in a large bowl and stir well. Add the meat and, using your hands, mix well until completely blended.

3. Put a sheet of heavy-duty foil, about 18 × 24 inches, on a work surface. Place a second sheet of equal size over the first and spray the top sheet lightly with vegetable oil cooking spray.

4. Place the meat mixture on the top sheet of foil and form into a compact rectangular loaf about 5 × 8 inches. Join the sides of the top sheet of foil over the meat and fold to make a secure package. Move the package a half turn on the bottom sheet and fold this sheet again, but with the folds running in the other direction so that the meat is securely encased.

5. Set the package on the grill and cook for about 35 minutes. Using thick oven mitts or tongs, turn the package over and grill for about 25 minutes longer. If using a charcoal grill, add fresh coals to maintain the heat. When ready, the meat will feel firm through the foil. Unwrap the meatloaf and using 2 spatulas transfer it to a serving platter. Slice into 1-inch-thick pieces for serving.

For this recipe, use either rib or loin veal chops. Rib chops are cut from the rib roast and because butchers do not have as many requests for rib roasts of veal as they do for chops, they very often cut the roasts into sizable, delicious chops. Loin veal chops have a large eye (meaty section), a tenderloin, and T-bone. Veal chops are among those cuts of meat that we feel benefit from the adage "less is more" and require neither a marinade nor much seasoning. We suggest serving these with a wine sauce to dress up the party.

Classic Grilled Veal Chops   *Serves 4*

FOUR 12-OUNCE RIB OR LOIN VEAL
    CHOPS, ABOUT 1 1/2 INCHES THICK
OLIVE OIL
SALT AND FRESHLY GROUND BLACK
    PEPPER TO TASTE
FOUR TOOTHPICKS OR SMALL METAL
    SKEWERS
VEGETABLE OIL COOKING SPRAY
MERLOT WINE SAUCE (PAGE 177)
    (OPTIONAL)

1. Rub the chops with oil and season on both sides with salt and pepper. Secure the tails of the chops to the thicker section of meat with toothpicks or small metal skewers, if necessary.

2. Prepare a charcoal or gas grill. Lightly spray the grill rack with vegetable oil cooking spray. The coals should be moderately hot.

3. Grill the chops for 8 to 10 minutes on each side until lightly browned for medium-rare. Serve with the sauce, if desired.

For this recipe, buy top round of veal and ask the butcher to slice it across the grain and then flatten it for you so that it is about a quarter of an inch thick. You will note that we use double skewers to hold the meat and vegetables securely in place . This is not necessary for all brochettes but does make turning them easier. (Use this technique in any recipe calling for skewers.) In this instance, the veal is cut into thin strips and woven on the skewers, so two skewers are necessary.

Veal and Mushroom Brochettes with Fresh Sage   *Serves 6*

2 POUNDS VEAL TOP ROUND, TRIMMED AND POUNDED TO AN EVEN THICKNESS OF ABOUT 1/4 INCH

1 POUND BROAD-CAPPED CREMINI MUSHROOMS, STEMMED (ABOUT 36 MUSHROOMS)

1/4 CUP FINELY CHOPPED SCALLIONS

1/4 CUP CHOPPED FRESH SAGE

2 TABLESPOONS FINELY CHOPPED LEMON ZEST

3 TABLESPOONS FRESH LEMON JUICE

2 TABLESPOONS OLIVE OIL

1/2 TEASPOON SALT

1/2 TEASPOON FRESHLY GROUND BLACK PEPPER

TWENTY-FOUR 12-INCH SKEWERS

VEGETABLE OIL COOKING SPRAY

1. Cut the veal into 24 strips about 4 inches long and 2 inches wide. Put in a glass or ceramic bowl. Add the mushrooms, scallions, sage, lemon zest, lemon juice, olive oil, salt, and pepper and toss gently to mix. Coat and refrigerate for at least 30 minutes and as long as 2 hours.

2. Soak twenty-four 12-inch bamboo skewers in cold water to cover for at least 20 minutes. Drain just before using.

3. Prepare a charcoal or gas grill. Lightly spray the grill rack with vegetable oil cooking spray. The coals should be moderately hot.

4. Thread the veal and mushrooms on the skewers, using 2 skewers at a time. Hold the skewers about 1/2 inch apart and thread a mushroom on the skewers, pushing it so that it is about 2 inches from the bottom of the skewers. Weave a strip of veal onto the skewers and then thread another mushroom on the skewers. Repeat with the remaining skewers and veal and mushrooms so that each 2-skewer brochette holds 2 strips of veal and 3 mushrooms.

5. Grill the brochettes for 6 to 8 minutes, turning once or twice, until the veal is medium-rare. Serve immediately.

CHAPTER 4

LAMB AND PORK

More and more, backyard cooks are turning to lamb and pork when deciding what to grill. Both are delicious when cooked over an open fire and both, being sweet-tasting meats, lend themselves to any number of marinades, rubs, sauces, and seasonings. Butterflied leg of lamb, marinated in a heady garlic-infused brew and then grilled, has become something of an American classic. Believe us, grilled pork tenderloin is not far behind in popularity.

At Lobel's, we sell only prime lamb and #1-grade pork. If possible, buy these top grades for the most tender and flavorful meat, or the best you can find. Most important is to find a butcher you trust, and who can make suggestions.

Both lamb and pork are meats from young animals, rarely more than a year old and generally far younger. You may have heard the term "baby lamb," which means just that: very young lamb that is between four and six weeks old, never weighs more than fifteen pounds, and has very tender, pale-pink meat. Few butchers carry baby lamb and if they do, it is only in the spring of the year. It is possible to buy lamb younger even than baby lamb. This is called a "hothouse lamb" and is only one or two weeks old. These lambs have had nothing but mother's milk and their meat is so tender you can cut it with a fork. However, even butchers who can special-order baby lamb cannot always get hothouse lamb and we consider it rare.

Most lamb is six to eight months old and weighs about thirty-five pounds. This means that the meat is pink, firm, and lean; the external fat is firm, white, and not too thick; and the bones are moist and healthfully red. Never buy lamb with dark red meat, yellowish fat, or pure white bones; these indicate older animals whose texture will be tough and the flavor overly intense.

People have been eating pork longer than any other domesticated animal. This may explain why so many ancient dietary restrictions grew up around pork, but it may also explain why we have such an abiding fondness for this rich-tasting, sweet meat. Today, more than 20 percent of the meat eaten by American consumers is pork, and a growing percentage of that is being cooked on the grill. Pork is graded differently from beef, veal, and lamb. Instead of being labeled as prime, choice, or good, pork is graded as #1, #2, and #3. If your butcher sells #1-grade pork, you are in luck. The pork will have pinkish-gray, lean meat and the fat will be firm and white. The bones should have red running through them to indicate blood and a young animal. With the exception of suckling pigs, most hogs are about 6 months old and weigh just over 200 pounds. Avoid pork with deep red meat, a coarse texture, bright white bones, and fat that appears yellow.

When grilling lamb or pork, remember that cooking times provided in our recipes are not exact. All grills cook a little differently, and some fires burn hotter than others. You will soon get to know your own grill and your own style and will be able to use our cooking times as guidelines. Test for doneness by looking at the meat (or by touch), and particularly with pork, use an instant-read thermometer to determine when the meat is done. Lamb can be served rare or better done (140°F for rare meat), but pork must be cooked thoroughly. The thermometer should register between 150° and 155°F. At this time, take the pork off the grill and let it rest for several minutes. During resting time, the internal temperature will rise to 160°F. This way, the meat will not overcook and be dry.

Preparing Lamb and Pork for Grilling

When you get the meat home from the butcher or supermarket, immediately stow it in the coldest part of the refrigerator, which usually is the rear of the lowest shelf. Do not unwrap it; you do not want to expose it to the air unnecessarily, and keeping it wrapped in its original packaging is a good idea.

When you are ready to prepare the meat, take it from the refrigerator and let it come to room temperature, which means leaving it on the counter for about 30 minutes. If it is a particularly hot, humid summer day, reduce the counter time by a few minutes. Pat the meat dry with paper towels and then either marinate it, rub it with dry rub, or otherwise prepare it for the grill. We have not always included this important step in the recipe instructions, because it is universally appropriate for all recipes calling for beef, veal, poultry, lamb, or pork to pat the meat dry with paper towels before cooking. If the meat is dry prior to cooking, it will brown nicely.

Buying Boned Leg of Lamb and Butterflied Leg of Lamb

Not all boned leg of lamb is "butterflied." Once the leg bone has been removed, the meat can either be rolled for roasting or butterflied for grilling. To ensure that you are buying a butterflied leg of lamb, ask the butcher specifically for it, and ask him to "butterfly it at both ends." One end is the top round end; the other end is the sirloin end. Both create a flap, which can then be flattened to even out and open up the meat. However, regardless of the skill of the butcher, all butterflied legs of lamb are imperfectly shaped by nature, which means that when grilling you have to tend to the meat carefully to ensure that it does not overcook.

Buying Meat in Season

Very few shoppers think of meat as being seasonal and while it is not as true as it once was, some types of meat are better at different times of year. Because of old-time farming practices, fresh pork used to be most available in the late fall, while lamb was reserved for the spring. Such strictures are not as clear nowadays, but some meats can be considered seasonal. Still, with modern farming, all meats and poultry are quite good year 'round.

Without question, lamb is at its best from mid April through October. Pork is tastiest from May until early October. Venison is best from October through December. Pheasant taste better when bought in the autumn, although they are quite good all year. Beef, veal, and quail are excellent all year long.

Buying Lamb Chops

Nowadays lamb chops are considered a great treat and so it's important to know what you're buying to get the most for your money. Without question, we prefer loin or rib chops. The meat in both chops is tender and flavorful and they grill beautifully. A two-inch-thick loin chop weighs about seven ounces and a one-and-one-half-inch-thick loin chop weighs about five ounces. However, we recommend that you buy chops according to thickness, not weight. Loin chops sold by butchers sometimes have longer tail bones than those sold in supermarkets, which can affect the weight and consequently the price.

Loin chops are from the loin of the lamb. Rib chops are those chops that, when attached, make up the rack (as in "rack of lamb" or "rack roast"). Loin chops have a small T-bone that separates the tenderloin from the eye. Some butchers insert a kidney below the tenderloin and curve the tail around it, securing it with a skewer; this is very fancy and not too common in this day of impersonal butcher counters. When loin chops are boned, trimmed, and rolled they are called "noisettes." Rib chops, which can be used whenever loin chops are called for, do not have tenderloins but are just as flavorful.

Other lamb chops are from the shoulder, and include both the blade and the arm chops. Blade shoulder chops are cut from the beginning of the shoulder, right after the rack, and are more desirable than arm shoulder chops. Arm shoulder chops are from the lower part of the shoulder, near the shank, and have a small round bone. These chops are less tender than the loin and rib chops but have good lamb flavor. They are less expensive and take well to marinating.

Buy It Cold, Cook It at Room Temperature

Always buy cold meat and poultry. In supermarkets, meat is stored in refrigerated cases and in butcher shops some is displayed in chilled cases, but most is held in the meat locker. When shopping for groceries, buy the meat last and when you get home, unpack it first and transfer it directly to the refrigerator or freezer. Remember that summer humidity and higher temperatures are hard on meats, so in warm weather, plan to grill the meat soon.

Keep the meat or poultry in the refrigerator almost until you are ready to cook it. You may have taken it from the refrigerator to marinate or rub it with a seasoning mix, but we advise returning it to cold storage as soon as it has been prepped. It is simply not safe to hold meat or poultry at room temperature.

However, there is one important exception to this rule: Meat should be at room temperature before you cook it. Take it from the refrigerator about thirty minutes before you are ready to grill. In the summertime, the meat may only need fifteen or twenty minutes to come to cool room temperature. As soon as the chill is gone, put the meat on the grill. If for some reason your timetable changes, return the uncooked meat to the refrigerator.

Should You Use Metal or Bamboo Skewers?

Use whichever type of skewers you prefer. Metal skewers get very hot on the grill and have to be handled carefully with oven mitts and long-handled tongs, but they are reusable, lasting virtually forever. Bamboo skewers are esthetically pleasing to many people, and when you are grilling numerous kabobs or short kabobs, they may be preferred because they are inexpensive and disposable. Bamboo skewers must be soaked in cool water for at least twenty or thirty minutes, or until they are saturated. They must then be drained just before the food is threaded on them. This helps prevent the bamboo from scorching on the grill.

Leg of lamb is a popular cut, one that most lamb lovers adore, and when the tip end of the shank is removed and the leg completely boned, the leg becomes a butterflied leg of lamb. Lay the meat out flat and you will note that although it is not uniformly even, its thickest parts are thin enough to grill nicely. You may choose to pound the thicker parts so that the entire piece of meat will cook more evenly.

Classic Grilled Butterflied Leg of Lamb with Garlicky Grilled Eggplant *Serves 6*

LAMB

1 CUP DRY RED WINE

1/2 CUP OLIVE OIL

2 LARGE CLOVES GARLIC, CHOPPED

3 TABLESPOONS CHOPPED FRESH THYME

1 1/2 TEASPOONS CRACKED BLACK PEPPER

1 TEASPOON SALT

ONE 4- TO 5-POUND BUTTERFLIED LEG OF LAMB

FRESHLY GROUND BLACK PEPPER TO TASTE

1/3 CUP EXTRA-VIRGIN OLIVE OIL

1 LARGE CLOVE GARLIC, CRUSHED

VEGETABLE OIL COOKING SPRAY

1. To prepare the lamb, combine the wine, oil, garlic, thyme, pepper, and salt in a glass or ceramic bowl and whisk well.

2. Put the lamb in a shallow glass or ceramic dish and pour the marinade over it, turning several times to coat. Cover and refrigerate for at least 6 hours and up to 24 hours.

3. To prepare the eggplant, about 1 hour before grilling, trim the eggplant and cut into 1/2-inch-thick slices. Sprinkle both sides of the slices generously with coarse salt, place them between sheets of paper towels, and set aside for about 30 minutes. Turn them once or twice. Rinse well under cool running water and pat dry. Set aside.

4. Combine the olive oil and minced garlic in a small bowl. Brush the eggplant generously on both sides and set aside in a shallow dish for about 30 minutes.

5. Prepare a charcoal or gas grill, arranging the coals for indirect cooking. Lightly spray the grill rack with vegetable oil cooking spray. The coals should be hot.

EGGPLANT

2 LARGE EGGPLANT

COARSE SALT TO TASTE

½ CUP OLIVE OIL

3 CLOVES GARLIC, MINCED

6. Lift the lamb from the marinade, pat dry, and season the lamb on both sides with freshly ground black pepper. Discard the marinade.

7. Combine the oil and crushed garlic in a small bowl for brushing on the meat.

8. Sear the lamb over the hot coals for about 5 minutes on each side, brushing with the olive oil and garlic mixture several times. Move the lamb to the cooler part of the grill, cover, and cook for about 10 minutes. Turn the meat over, cover, and cook for 10 to 15 minutes longer for medium-rare meat, or until cooked to desired doneness. An instant-read thermometer inserted in the thickest part of the meat should register 140°F for rare meat and 145° to 150°F for medium-rare. Continue brushing the lamb with the remaining olive oil and garlic mixture during the first 20 minutes of grilling. Let the lamb rest for about 10 minutes before slicing.

9. About 10 minutes before the lamb is done, cook the eggplant on the edge of the grill, away from the hottest part of the fire, for about 4 minutes. Turn and cook for about 5 minutes longer, or until tender. Serve with the lamb.

Lamb and yogurt is a match made in heaven, and when mixed with garlic, mint, and fresh thyme, the perfect combination just gets better. With flavorful marinades such as those we suggest with lamb, you won't miss gravy made from pan juices. Butterflied leg of lamb is an uneven piece of meat and so you will have to adjust the cooking time or pound sections of the lamb to promote even cooking.

Butterflied Leg of Lamb Marinated in Yogurt and Mint *Serves 6*

1 CUP PLAIN YOGURT

2 TABLESPOONS FRESH LEMON JUICE

1 TABLESPOON OLIVE OIL

4 SCALLIONS, FINELY CHOPPED

3 LARGE CLOVES GARLIC, MINCED, PLUS 1 LARGE CLOVE GARLIC

¼ CUP CHOPPED FRESH MINT

2 TABLESPOONS CHOPPED FRESH THYME

GRATED ZEST OF 1 LEMON

1 TABLESPOON CRACKED BLACK PEPPER

SALT TO TASTE

ONE 4- TO 5-POUND BUTTERFLIED LEG OF LAMB

VEGETABLE OIL COOKING SPRAY

⅓ CUP EXTRA-VIRGIN OLIVE OIL

1 LARGE CLOVE GARLIC, CRUSHED

1. Combine the yogurt, lemon juice, olive oil, scallions, minced garlic, mint, thyme, lemon zest, pepper, and salt in a large bowl and stir to mix.

2. Rub the garlic clove over both sides of the lamb and put the lamb in a shallow glass or ceramic dish. Pour the marinade over the meat and turn it several times to coat. Cover and refrigerate for 4 to 6 hours. About 30 minutes before grilling, remove the meat from the refrigerator and let it come to room temperature.

3. Prepare a charcoal or gas grill arranging the coals for indirect cooking. Lightly spray the grill rack with vegetable oil cooking spray. The coals should be hot.

4. Lift the lamb from the marinade, scrape off the excess marinade, and season both sides with salt and pepper. Discard the marinade.

5. Combine the oil and crushed garlic in a small bowl for brushing on the meat.

6. Sear the lamb over the hot coals for about 5 minutes on each side, brushing with the olive oil and garlic mixture several times; continue brushing the lamb with the remaining olive oil and garlic mixture during the first 20 minutes of grilling. Move the lamb to the cooler part of the grill, cover, and cook for about 10 minutes. Turn the meat over, cover, and cook for 10 to 15 minutes longer for medium-rare meat, or until cooked to desired doneness. An instant-read thermometer inserted in the thickest part of the meat should register 140°F for rare meat and 145° to 150°F for medium-rare. Let the lamb rest for about 10 minutes before slicing.

Butterflied leg of lamb is not a pretty sight when you bring it home. It's a lumpy piece of meat, often folded back on itself and one that frequently requires trimming and gentle flattening.

Butterflied Leg of Lamb with Cumin and Garlic *Serves 6*

2 TABLESPOONS FRESH LEMON JUICE

2 TABLESPOONS GROUND CUMIN

3 LARGE CLOVES GARLIC, MINCED

FRESHLY GROUND BLACK PEPPER TO
   TASTE

ONE 4- TO 5-POUND BUTTERFLIED LEG
   OF LAMB

VEGETABLE OIL COOKING SPRAY

⅓ CUP EXTRA-VIRGIN OLIVE OIL

1 LARGE CLOVE GARLIC, CRUSHED

1. Combine the lemon juice, cumin, garlic, and pepper in a small bowl and stir into a paste.

2. Put the lamb in a shallow glass or ceramic dish and rub both sides with the garlic-cumin paste. Cover and refrigerate for 4 to 6 hours. About 30 minutes before grilling, remove the meat from the refrigerator and let it come to room temperature.

3. Prepare a charcoal or gas grill, arranging the coals for indirect cooking. Lightly spray the grill rack with vegetable oil cooking spray. The coals should be hot.

4. Combine the oil and crushed garlic in a small dish for brushing on the meat.

5. Sear the lamb over the hot coals for about 5 minutes on each side, brushing with the olive oil and garlic mixture several times. Move the lamb to the cooler part of the grill, cover, and cook for about 10 minutes. Turn the meat, cover, and cook for 10 to 15 minutes longer for medium-rare meat, or until cooked to desired doneness. An instant-read thermometer inserted in the thickest part of the meat should register 140°F for rare meat and 145 to 150°F for medium-rare. Continue brushing the lamb with the remaining olive oil and garlic mixture during grilling. Let the lamb rest for about 10 minutes before slicing.

Lamb chops are small, juicy, utterly irresistible treasures. Loin chops are deliciously tender and have a small T-bone that separates the tenderloin from the eye. The double loin (both sides of the animal) is called the saddle. When the saddle is cut into individual double chops, the chops are called "English lamb chops." In this instance, the tails of the chops are tucked around the tenderloin to form a circle of meat—so there are two T-bones and two tenderloins. Most likely the English recognized that a double loin chop was twice as good as a single! Rib chops match loin chops when it comes to flavor and tenderness. These are the chops from a rack of lamb and while they have no tenderloin, they are tasty.

Mint-Brushed Lamb Chops   *Serves 6*

½ CUP CIDER VINEGAR

2 TEASPOONS SUGAR

½ CUP COARSELY CHOPPED FRESH
    MINT

12 LOIN OR RIB LAMB CHOPS, ABOUT
    2 INCHES THICK

VEGETABLE OIL COOKING SPRAY

FRESHLY GROUND BLACK PEPPER TO
    TASTE

1. Combine the vinegar and sugar in a small bowl and stir until the sugar dissolves. Transfer to a blender and add the mint. Blend until the mint is finely chopped. Brush on both sides of the chops and set aside at room temperature for about 10 minutes. Reserve some of the mixture to brush on the chops during grilling.

2. Prepare a charcoal or gas grill. Lightly spray the grill rack with vegetable oil cooking spray. The coals should be moderately hot to hot.

3. Grill the chops for 6 to 8 minutes on each side until medium-rare, or cooked to desired degree of doneness. Watch for flare-ups. Move the chops to a cooler part of the grill and extinguish the flames with a spray of water. If they occur, move the chops back to the hot fire. Baste with the vinegar mixture several times during grilling. Season with pepper just before serving.

For this recipe we use loin or rib chops for their tenderness and sweet flavor. However, you could substitute shoulder lamb chops, which, while not as tender, are less expensive and quite flavorful.

Lamb Chops with Grilled Stuffed Mushrooms

Serves 4

LAMB CHOPS

2 CLOVES GARLIC, CRUSHED

¼ CUP PLUS 2 TABLESPOONS FINELY
   GRATED ONION (SEE NOTE)

1½ TEASPOONS FRESHLY GROUND
   BLACK PEPPER

1 TEASPOON CHOPPED FRESH
   ROSEMARY

1 TEASPOON CHOPPED FRESH THYME

½ TEASPOON SALT

8 LOIN OR RIB LAMB CHOPS, ABOUT
   1½ INCHES THICK

¼ CUP OLIVE OIL

¼ CUP DRY RED WINE

VEGETABLE OIL COOKING SPRAY

1. To prepare the chops, combine the garlic, onion, pepper, rosemary, thyme, and salt in a small bowl and stir into a paste. Rub the paste into both sides of the chops. Put the chops in a large glass or ceramic dish, pour the oil and wine over them, turning the chops to coat. Cover and refrigerate at least 2 hours or overnight.

2. Prepare a charcoal or gas grill. Lightly spray the grill rack with vegetable oil cooking spray. The coals should be moderately hot to hot.

3. To prepare the mushrooms, combine the feta, cream cheese, parsley, thyme, and marjoram in a small bowl, season with pepper, and mix well.

4. Remove the stems from the mushrooms, leaving a cavity in the cap. Rub the caps inside and out with oil and sprinkle lightly with salt. Put the mushrooms on the grill, cavity side down, and grill for 2 or 3 minutes, or until lightly browned and softened. Transfer the mushrooms to a pan, cavity side up, and spoon an equal amount of the cheese filling in each.

5. Lift the chops from the marinade and let the marinade drip back into the dish. Grill the chops for 6 or 8 minutes on each side until medium-rare, or cooked to desired degree of doneness.

MUSHROOMS

$3/4$ CUP CRUMBLED FETA CHEESE
(ABOUT 4 OUNCES)

$1/4$ CUP CREAM CHEESE, SOFTENED

2 TABLESPOONS CHOPPED FRESH FLAT-
LEAF PARSLEY

$1/2$ TEASPOON CHOPPED FRESH THYME

$1/2$ TEASPOON CRUSHED DRIED MARJO-
RAM

FRESHLY GROUND BLACK PEPPER TO
TASTE

TWENTY-FOUR 2-INCH-DIAMETER
WHITE OR CREMINI MUSHROOMS

OLIVE OIL

SALT TO TASTE

6. Just before turning the chops, put the mushrooms filled side up on the edge of the grill, away from the hottest part of the fire, and cook for 5 or 6 minutes, or until the cheese begins to melt. Remove the mushrooms and the chops from the grill and serve them together.

note: To grate the onion, rub the cut portion of the onion along a hand-held cheese grater or grate the onion in a food processor.

Rosemary is perhaps the herb that best brings out the flavor of lamb, and while we usually prefer fresh rosemary, for this recipe, we like the dried herb. We call for loin or rib chops for this and a number of other recipes in the book. Rib chops are the same chops that make up a rack roast. They have no tenderloin but their meat is succulent and tasty. The rack roast can be cut into single, double, or triple chops. When the fat is trimmed and the end of the bone is left bare so that the meat resembles a small circle attached to the bone, the chops are called "French rib lamb chops"—and sometimes a paper frill is slipped over the bone to disguise it. However, when we grill chops, we leave the frilly decorations inside the house!

Grilled Loin Lamb Chops with Rosemary   *Serves 6*

½ CUP OLIVE OIL

¼ CUP RED WINE VINEGAR

2 TABLESPOONS DRIED ROSEMARY

2 CLOVES GARLIC, MINCED

12 RIB OR LOIN LAMB CHOPS, ABOUT
   1½ INCHES THICK

VEGETABLE OIL COOKING SPRAY

SALT AND FRESHLY GROUND BLACK
   PEPPER TO TASTE

1. Combine olive oil, vinegar, rosemary, and garlic in a small bowl. Put the chops in a shallow glass or ceramic dish and add the marinade, turning the chops several times to coat. Cover and refrigerate for 4 hours or overnight.

2. Prepare a charcoal or gas grill. Lightly spray the grill rack with vegetable oil cooking spray. The coals should be moderately hot to hot.

3. Grill the chops for about 6 to 8 minutes on each side for medium-rare lamb, or until cooked to desired degree of doneness. Season with salt and pepper and serve.

In butcher-shop terminology, lambs don't have front legs. There are back legs and there are shoulders. Shoulder meat is not as tender as leg and loin and rib meat, and therefore is less expensive. Blade lamb chops are cut from the top of the shoulder, right after the rack, and arm lamb chops are cut from lower in the shoulder, near the shank. Arm chops have a small round bone near their centers. Both are great on the grill, particularly if flavored boldly, as these are with mustard and cumin.

Mustard-Glazed Shoulder Lamb Chops   *Serves 6*

VEGETABLE OIL COOKING SPRAY

2 TABLESPOONS DIJON MUSTARD

2 TABLESPOONS RED WINE VINEGAR

2 TEASPOONS GROUND CUMIN

FRESHLY GROUND BLACK PEPPER TO
TASTE

12 SHOULDER LAMB CHOPS, ABOUT 1
INCH THICK

1. Prepare a charcoal or gas grill. Lightly spray the grill rack with vegetable oil cooking spray. The coals should be moderately hot to hot.

2. Combine the mustard, vinegar, cumin, and pepper in a small bowl. Brush on the chops and marinate at room temperature for 10 to 20 minutes.

3. Grill the chops for 5 to 6 minutes on each side until medium-rare, or cooked to desired degree of doneness. Season with pepper just before serving.

A rack is a connected series of rib chops. The butcher usually cracks the bones so that the rack is easy to separate into chops after cooking. For some reason, home cooks regard racks of lamb as too fancy to grill—which couldn't be farther from the truth. A rack lends itself to grilling as readily as do separate chops—and it looks magnificent when lifted from the grill, perfectly browned and just a little crusty.

Simple Grilled Rack of Lamb *Serves 6 to 8*

2 RACKS OF LAMB (8 CHOPS EACH,
    EACH RACK ABOUT 1¾ POUNDS)
¼ CUP PLUS 2 TABLESPOONS OLIVE
    OIL
1 TABLESPOON CHOPPED FRESH
    ROSEMARY
FRESHLY GROUND BLACK PEPPER TO
    TASTE
VEGETABLE OIL COOKING SPRAY

1. Trim the lamb, if necessary, and rub both sides of the rack with olive oil. Sprinkle with rosemary and pepper, rubbing them into the meatiest parts of the racks.

2. Prepare a charcoal or gas grill. Lightly spray the grill rack with vegetable oil cooking spray. The coals should be moderately hot to hot.

3. Grill the racks, meat side down, for 4 or 5 minutes, or until the temperature of the meatiest part reaches 100°F. Move the racks to the edge of the grill, away from the hottest part of the fire, and cook, covered, for 15 to 20 minutes longer, or until the temperature reaches 140°F for rare meat. Remove the racks from the grill and let them rest for about 5 minutes before cutting between the ribs into individual chops.

We like to rub rack of lamb with a heady mixture of blue cheese, rosemary, and garlic before grilling it. The resulting meat is boldly flavored and absolutely delicious.

Rack of Lamb Rubbed with Blue Cheese

Serves 8

2 RACKS OF LAMB (8 CHOPS EACH, EACH RACK ABOUT 1³/₄ POUNDS)

¹/₄ CUP PLUS 2 TABLESPOONS OLIVE OIL

2 HEAPING TABLESPOONS CRUMBLED BLUE CHEESE

2 TABLESPOONS MUSTARD SEEDS

4 TEASPOONS MASHED GARLIC

2 TEASPOONS CHOPPED FRESH ROSEMARY

FRESHLY GROUND BLACK PEPPER TO TASTE

VEGETABLE OIL COOKING SPRAY

1. Trim the lamb, if necessary. Combine the oil, blue cheese, mustard seeds, garlic, and rosemary in a small bowl, season with pepper, and stir to make a paste. Spread the paste on the racks, rubbing it into the meatiest parts of the racks.

2. Prepare a charcoal or gas grill. Lightly spray the grill rack with vegetable oil cooking spray. The coals should be moderately hot to hot.

3. Grill the racks, meat side down, for 4 or 5 minutes, or until the temperature of the meatiest part reaches 100°F. Move the racks to the edge of the grill, away from the most intense heat and grill, covered, for 10 to 15 minutes longer or until the temperature reaches 140°F for medium-rare meat. Lift the racks from the grill and let them rest for about 5 minutes before cutting between the ribs into individual chops.

Some butchers cut meat for kabobs from nearly any part of the lamb, but we feel that the best meat for skewered, grilled lamb comes from the leg. If the butcher hasn't done so, trim the meat well to ensure that no tough membranes remain.

Lamb Kabobs Marinated in Red Wine   *Serves 6*

1 CUP DRY RED WINE

¼ CUP OLIVE OIL

2 TO 3 SCALLIONS, CHOPPED

2 LARGE CLOVES GARLIC, MINCED

2 TABLESPOONS CHOPPED FLAT-LEAF
  PARSLEY

1 TABLESPOON CHOPPED FRESH
  ROSEMARY

SALT AND FRESHLY CRACKED BLACK
  PEPPER TO TASTE

3 POUNDS BONELESS LEG OF LAMB,
  TRIMMED AND CUT INTO 1½-INCH
  CUBES

VEGETABLE OIL COOKING SPRAY

1 SMALL ONION, CUT INTO 6 WEDGES

12 LARGE WHITE MUSHROOMS (ABOUT
  ½ POUND), STEMMED

12 CHERRY TOMATOES

SIX 12-INCH METAL SKEWERS

1. Combine the wine, oil, scallions, garlic, parsley, and rosemary in a glass or ceramic bowl; season to taste with salt and pepper. Add the lamb, toss to coat, cover, and refrigerate for 4 hours or overnight.

2. Prepare a charcoal or gas grill. Lightly spray the grill rack with vegetable oil cooking spray. The coals should be moderately hot to hot.

3. Thread the lamb, onion wedges, mushrooms, and tomatoes onto skewers, beginning and ending with meat. Grill for 8 to 10 minutes, turning several times with tongs and brushing 2 or 3 times with the marinade during the first few minutes of grilling. Cook until the lamb is medium-rare and the vegetables are tender. Serve immediately.

The front section of the hindsaddle of the lamb is the sirloin, which is the thickest part of the leg. The rear section of hindsaddle is the shank. A whole leg of lamb includes both the sirloin and the shank. The two sections can be separated for a sirloin leg of lamb and a shank leg of lamb. Meat for kabobs can come from either section, with the sirloin obviously being a little more tender.

Lamb Kabobs with Garam Masala and Yogurt Marinade   *Serves 6*

1 CUP PLAIN YOGURT

¼ CUP FRESH LEMON JUICE

2 CLOVES GARLIC, MINCED OR
   CRUSHED THROUGH A PRESS

2 TABLESPOONS MINCED FRESH
   GINGER

1 TABLESPOON GARAM MASALA (PAGE
   197; SEE NOTE)

2 TEASPOONS SUGAR

1 TEASPOON GROUND CUMIN

1 TEASPOON SALT

¼ TEASPOON GROUND CAYENNE

3 POUNDS BONELESS LEG OF LAMB,
   TRIMMED AND CUT INTO 1½-INCH
   CUBES

VEGETABLE OIL COOKING SPRAY

SIX 12-INCH METAL SKEWERS

1. Combine the yogurt, lemon juice, garlic, ginger, garam masala, sugar, cumin, salt, and cayenne in a large glass or ceramic bowl. Add the lamb, toss to coat, cover, and refrigerate for 4 hours or overnight.

2. Prepare a charcoal or gas grill. Lightly spray the grill rack with vegetable oil cooking spray. The coals should be moderately hot to hot.

3. Thread 4 or 5 pieces of lamb on six skewers. Discard the marinade. Grill for 8 to 10 minutes, turning several times with tongs, until the lamb is medium-rare. Serve immediately.

note: Garam masala is sold in Indian markets and specialty food stores. We have a recipe for making your own on page 197 and while it may seem like a lot of trouble, it keeps for months.

When you cut meat into cubes for kabobs, make sure you cut them into good-sized cubes, at least 1½ inches thick. These are large enough to hold up to grilling and to not fall through the grill rack if one slips off the skewer. For sturdy kabobs that are easy to turn, lay two skewers next to each other and thread the meat and vegetables on both. The food cannot twist on the skewers. You will need twice the number of skewers called for in the recipe.

South India-Style Lamb Kabobs   *Serves 6*

¾ CUP CANOLA OIL

2 CLOVES GARLIC, MINCED

2 TABLESPOONS GRATED FRESH GINGER

1 TABLESPOON GROUND CORIANDER

2 TEASPOONS GROUND CUMIN

PINCH GROUND CINNAMON

PINCH GROUND CARDAMOM

3 POUNDS BONELESS LEG OF LAMB, TRIMMED AND CUT INTO 1½-INCH CUBES

SALT AND FRESHLY GROUND BLACK PEPPER TO TASTE

VEGETABLE OIL COOKING SPRAY

1 SMALL ONION, CUT INTO 6 WEDGES

1 LARGE GREEN BELL PEPPER, CUT INTO 1½-INCH CHUNKS

1 LARGE RED BELL PEPPER, CUT INTO 1½-INCH CHUNKS

SIX 12-INCH METAL SKEWERS

1. Combine the oil, garlic, ginger, coriander, cumin, cinnamon, and cardamom in a large glass or ceramic dish. Sprinkle the lamb generously with salt and pepper and add the lamb to the marinade. Toss to coat, cover, and refrigerate for at least 2 hours and as long as 6 hours.

2. Prepare a charcoal or gas grill. Lightly spray the grill rack with vegetable oil cooking spray. The coals should be moderately hot to hot.

3. Thread the lamb, onion wedges, and peppers onto skewers, beginning and ending with the meat. Grill for 8 to 10 minutes, turning several times with tongs and brushing 2 or 3 times with any excess marinade during the first few minutes of grilling. Cook until the lamb is medium-rare and the vegetables are tender. Serve immediately.

The best lamb steaks are cut from the leg, where the meat is finely textured and full of good lamb flavor. It makes sense, when buying a whole leg of lamb, to ask the butcher to cut a few steaks from the sirloin end to use for grilling. However, any good butcher will cut lamb steaks for you if you ask. Because these steaks are quite large, they are cut relatively thin. These steaks are also called "leg lamb chops."

Lamb Steaks with Lemon and Parsley
Serves 6

6 LAMB STEAKS, 1¼-INCH-THICK, CUT
  FROM THE LEG (2½ TO 3 POUNDS)
CRACKED BLACK PEPPER TO TASTE
3 TABLESPOONS OLIVE OIL
GRATED ZEST OF 1 LEMON
JUICE OF 2 LEMONS
3 TABLESPOONS CHOPPED FLAT-LEAF
  PARSLEY
VEGETABLE OIL COOKING SPRAY

1. Rub both sides of the lamb steaks with cracked pepper and put them in a shallow glass or ceramic dish.

2. Combine the oil, lemon zest, lemon juice, and parsley in a small bowl, stirring well, and add to the lamb, turning the steaks several times to coat. Cover and refrigerate for at least 4 hours and as long as 12 hours.

3. Prepare a charcoal or gas grill. Lightly spray the grill rack with vegetable oil cooking spray. The coals should be moderately hot to hot.

4. Lift the steaks from the marinade, reserving the marinade. Grill the steaks for 10 to 12 minutes, turning several times with tongs and brushing 2 or 3 times with the marinade during the first few minutes of cooking. Grill the lamb until it is medium-rare, or until it reaches desired degree of doneness.

Pull up a chair and dig in! Few offerings off the grill beat spareribs for plain, old-fashioned "good eats." The spareribs are the breast and rib bones from the lower part of the center section of the hog, with tender, lean meat tucked between the bones. Cooking times can vary wildly when cooking ribs—some are meatier than others—so keep a close watch to keep them from burning or drying out.

Western-Style Grilled Spareribs *Serves 6*

5 TO 6 POUNDS SPARERIBS (TWO
    2¹/₂- TO 3-POUND RACKS)
¹/₂ CUP PEPPERY DRY RUB (PAGE 193)
VEGETABLE OIL COOKING SPRAY
MADISON AVENUE BARBECUE SAUCE
    (PAGE 173)

1. Trim the spareribs, if necessary, and rub both sides of the ribs with the dry rub, working it into the meat. Put the ribs in a shallow glass or ceramic dish, cover, and set aside at room temperature for no longer than 30 minutes, or refrigerate for up to 24 hours. Alternatively, enclose the ribs in a sealable plastic bag and refrigerate.

2. Prepare a charcoal or gas grill, arranging the coals for indirect cooking. Lightly spray the grill rack with vegetable oil cooking spray. The coals should be hot.

3. Set the ribs, meat side down, over the hottest part of the fire and sear for about 10 minutes until there are defined grill marks on the meat. Transfer the ribs to the cooler part of the grill, cover, and turning the ribs every 15 to 20 minutes, cook for about 1¹/₂ hours. If using a charcoal grill, add fresh coals to maintain the heat at medium; if using a gas grill, turn the heat to medium on the burner away from the meat—turn off the burner under the meat. Cut the ribs between the bones and serve with sauce on the side.

A full slab of spareribs has thirteen ribs, but a rack, which indicates human manipulation, can have any number up to twelve, depending on how the butcher or chef prepares it. Most full slabs weigh from three to three and one-half pounds, so when you want enough ribs to feed at least six hungry people, you will have to buy at least two slabs—or twelve-rib racks.

Southeast Asian-Flavored Spareribs

Serves 6

5 TO 6 POUNDS SPARERIBS (TWO
2½- TO 3-POUND RACKS)
1 CUP ASIAN-STYLE LEMONGRASS
PASTE (PAGE 198)
VEGETABLE OIL COOKING SPRAY

1. Trim the spareribs, if necessary, and rub both sides of the ribs with the paste, working it into the meat. Put the ribs in a shallow glass or ceramic dish, cover, and set aside at room temperature for no longer than 30 minutes, or refrigerate for up to 24 hours. Alternatively, enclose the ribs in a sealable plastic bag and refrigerate.

2. Prepare a charcoal or gas grill, arranging the coals for indirect cooking. Lightly spray the grill rack with vegetable oil cooking spray. The coals should be hot.

3. Set the ribs, meat side down, over the hottest part of the fire and sear for about 10 minutes until there are defined grill marks on the meat. Transfer the ribs to the cooler part of the grill, cover, and turning the ribs every 15 to 20 minutes, cook for about 1½ hours. If using a charcoal grill, add fresh coals to maintain the heat at medium; if using a gas grill, turn the heat to medium on the burner away from the meat—turn off the burner under the meat. Cut the ribs between the bones and serve.

Country-style ribs—cut from the blade end of the loin and with no fewer than three and no more than six ribs in a rack—are much meatier than spareribs. You can make this recipe with spareribs. Whichever ribs you select, leave your indoor table manners behind and bring a good appetite to the feast.

Sweet Heat Country-Style Pork Ribs   *Serves 6 to 8*

2 VERY RIPE PAPAYAS, PEELED,
    SEEDED, AND COARSELY CHOPPED

1/2 CUP DRY WHITE WINE

1/4 CUP FRESH LIME JUICE

3 TABLESPOONS GRATED FRESH GINGER

2 TABLESPOONS SOY SAUCE

2 TEASPOONS CHINESE FIVE-SPICE
    POWDER

2 TEASPOONS HOT HUNGARIAN
    PAPRIKA

5 TO 6 POUNDS COUNTRY-STYLE PORK
    RIBS

VEGETABLE OIL COOKING SPRAY

1. Combine the papaya flesh, wine, lime juice, ginger, soy sauce, five-spice powder, and paprika in a food processor and pulse 4 or 5 times, or until smooth.

2. Put the ribs in a glass or ceramic dish large enough to hold them in a single layer and add the marinade, turning the ribs several times to coat. Cover and refrigerate for at least 4 hours and as long as 8 hours.

3. Prepare a charcoal or gas grill, arranging the coals for indirect cooking. Lightly spray the grill rack with vegetable oil cooking spray. The coals should be hot.

4. Lift the ribs from the marinade and scrape most of the marinade from them. Discard the marinade. Set the ribs, meat side down, over the hottest part of the fire and sear for about 10 minutes until there are defined grill marks on the meat. Transfer the ribs to the cooler part of the grill, cover, and turning the ribs every 15 to 20 minutes, cook for about $1^1/_2$ hours, or until a meat thermometer inserted in the meatiest part of the ribs registers 160°F. If using a charcoal grill, add fresh coals to maintain the heat at medium; if using a gas grill, turn the heat to medium on the burner away from the meat; turn off the burner under the meat. Cut the ribs between the bones and serve.

The slender tenderloin is cut from the front part of the center loin pork roast. We suggest grilling three loins for six people, which is generous. Once you taste this tender, sweet meat, you will be happy there is enough for seconds.

Pork Tenderloin Rubbed with Mustard and Bourbon

Serves 6

¾ CUP SPICY BROWN MUSTARD

¼ CUP PLUS 2 TABLESPOONS
BOURBON

3 TABLESPOONS OLIVE OIL

3 CLOVES GARLIC, MINCED

¼ CUP PLUS 2 TABLESPOONS
CHOPPED FRESH THYME

3 TABLESPOONS CHOPPED FLAT-LEAF
PARSLEY

FRESHLY GROUND BLACK PEPPER TO
TASTE

3 PORK TENDERLOINS (EACH ¾ TO 1
POUND), TRIMMED

VEGETABLE OIL COOKING SPRAY

1. Combine the mustard, bourbon, oil, garlic, thyme, parsley, and pepper in a bowl, stirring well. Rub into the tenderloins, covering the meat on all sides.

2. Put the tenderloins in a glass or ceramic dish, cover, and set aside at room temperature for no longer than 30 minutes, or refrigerate for as long as 4 hours. If they have been refrigerated, let the tenderloins stand at room temperature for about 15 minutes before grilling.

3. Prepare a charcoal or gas grill. Lightly spray the grill rack with vegetable oil cooking spray. The coals should be moderately hot to hot.

4. Grill the tenderloins for 12 to 14 minutes, turning with tongs once or twice, until cooked through and the internal temperature reaches 150° to 155°F. Let the pork rest for about 10 minutes before slicing; the temperature will rise to 160°F during the resting period. Slice thinly and serve.

One of the best ways to cook pork is on the grill. Even the succulent tenderloin shines when marinated with a full-bodied marinade and then grilled. Because you want to cook pork fully, use a reliable meat thermometer so that it will be perfect—but not overcooked.

Pork Tenderloin Marinated in Apple Cider   *Serves 6*

1 CUP APPLE CIDER OR APPLE JUICE

2 TO 3 TABLESPOONS RAISINS

2 TABLESPOONS BROWN SUGAR

1/4 TEASPOON CLOVES

1 TEASPOON GROUND CINNAMON

1/4 TEASPOON GROUND MACE

1/4 TEASPOON GROUND CARDAMOM

FRESHLY GROUND BLACK PEPPER TO TASTE

3 PORK TENDERLOINS (EACH 3/4 TO 1 POUND), TRIMMED

VEGETABLE OIL COOKING SPRAY

1. Combine the cider, raisins, brown sugar, cloves, cinnamon, mace, cardamom, and pepper in a small saucepan and bring to a boil over high heat. Reduce the heat to medium and cook, stirring, for 4 or 5 minutes, or until the flavors blend and the raisins plump slightly. Remove from the heat and let cool slightly.

2. Put the tenderloins in a shallow glass or ceramic dish and pour the marinade over them. Cover and set aside at room temperature for no longer than 30 minutes, or refrigerate for as long as 4 hours. If they have been refrigerated, let the tenderloins stand at room temperature for about 15 minutes before grilling.

3. Prepare a charcoal or gas grill. Lightly spray the grill rack with vegetable oil cooking spray. The coals should be moderately hot to hot.

4. Lift the tenderloins from the marinade, reserving the marinade. Grill the tenderloins for 14 to 17 minutes, turning with tongs once or twice and brushing with the marinade during the first 10 minutes of cooking. Grill the tenderloins until cooked through and the internal temperature reaches 150° to 155°F. Let the pork rest for about 10 minutes before slicing; the temperature will rise to 160°F during the resting period. Slice thinly and serve.

A boneless pork loin roast is the center loin roast with the ribs and T-bones removed. It may contain the tenderloin, although usually this has been cut out of the loin. If you have the option, remove the tenderloin and freeze it for up to a month for later grilling. It's important to use the meat thermometer when determining when pork is cooked. Take the meat from the grill when the thermometer registers 150° to 155°F. and then let it rest for a few minutes. The temperature will rise to 160°F. during resting. This avoids the possibility of overcooking.

Fiery Asian-Style Pork Loin Roast *Serves 6 to 8*

½ CUP ORANGE JUICE

2 TABLESPOONS FROZEN ORANGE JUICE CONCENTRATE

2 TABLESPOONS HONEY

1 TABLESPOON SOY SAUCE

1 TABLESPOON OLIVE OIL

1 TEASPOON MINCED GARLIC

1 TEASPOON MINCED FRESH GINGER

½ TEASPOON CHINESE FIVE-SPICE POWDER

1 TEASPOON ASIAN CHILI PASTE

2 TO 3 DROPS HOT CHILI OIL

ONE 4- TO 4½-POUND BONELESS PORK LOIN ROAST, TRIMMED

VEGETABLE OIL COOKING SPRAY

MINTED SUMMER FRUIT SALSA (PAGE 183) OR BAJA-STYLE TOMATO SALSA (PAGE 185) (OPTIONAL)

1. Combine the orange juice, juice concentrate, honey, soy sauce, oil, garlic, ginger, five-spice powder, chili paste, and chili oil in a bowl, stirring well.

2. Put the roast in a shallow glass or ceramic dish and pour the marinade over it. Turn to coat. Cover and refrigerate for at least 2 hours and as long as 12 hours.

3. Prepare a charcoal or gas grill, arranging the coals for indirect cooking. Lightly spray the grill rack with vegetable oil cooking spray. The coals should be moderately hot.

4. Lift the roast from the marinade, reserving the marinade and brushing it on the roast 2 or 3 times during the first 30 minutes of cooking. Grill over indirect heat with the grill covered for about 1 hour and 10 minutes, or until a meat thermometer inserted in the center of the roast registers 150° to 155°F. Remove the roast from the grill and let it rest for about 10 minutes before slicing. Serve with salsa, if desired.

Loin pork chops are cut from the front of the center loin and have a tasty nugget of tenderloin nestled next to the T-bone. They are juicy and delicious—a favorite for grilling. You could substitute rib pork chops, which are equally tasty but don't have the tenderloin. Beware of this spice rub: It is not for the faint of heart. The salsa cools it down a little, but not completely! If the rub is to your liking, try it on pork loin or spareribs, too.

Southwest-Style Pork Chops with Ancho Chili Powder   *Serves 4*

3 TABLESPOONS ANCHO CHILI POWDER
  (SEE NOTE)
1 TABLESPOON CRUSHED TOASTED
  CUMIN SEEDS (SEE NOTE)
1 TEASPOON CRUSHED TOASTED
  CORIANDER SEEDS (SEE NOTE)
1 TEASPOON DRY MUSTARD
SALT AND FRESHLY GROUND BLACK
  PEPPER TO TASTE
4 LOIN PORK CHOPS, ABOUT 1½
  INCHES THICK
VEGETABLE OIL COOKING SPRAY
BAJA-STYLE TOMATO SALSA (PAGE 185)

1. Combine the chili powder, cumin seeds, coriander seeds, and dry mustard in a small bowl. Season with salt and pepper, stirring well.

2. Rub the mixture into the meatiest parts of the pork chops and put the chops in a glass or ceramic dish. Cover and set aside at room temperature for about 30 minutes, or refrigerate for as long as 8 hours.

3. Prepare a charcoal or gas grill. Lightly spray the grill rack with vegetable oil cooking spray. The coals should be moderately hot.

4. Grill the chops for 8 to 10 minutes on each side, or until a meat thermometer inserted in the center of the meatiest sections registers 150° to 155°F. Let the chops rest for a few minutes before serving. Serve with the salsa.

note: Ancho chili powder is made from ground ancho chilies, which are mildly hot. The powder is stronger-tasting than other chili powders and is generally available in Hispanic and specialty markets. If you cannot find it, substitute any chili powder.

To toast the seeds, spread them in a small dry skillet and cook over medium-high heat for about 60 seconds or until fragrant. Crush the seeds with a skillet. Measure after crushing.

Pork chops, when cut nice and thick, lend themselves to grilling like no other chop. A lamb chop or veal chop can be ruined if overcooked, but a pork chop tolerates a little more abuse. Although care should be taken never to overcook it, it will not turn from rare and juicy to gray and tough in a blink as red meat does. We especially like blending pork with Asian spices and flavorings.

Asian-Marinated Pork Chops with Sesame Seeds   *Serves 4*

1/2 CUP SOY SAUCE

1/4 CUP MINCED SCALLIONS

2 TABLESPOONS PLUS 1 1/2 TEASPOONS
    LIGHT OR DARK BROWN SUGAR

2 TABLESPOONS TOASTED SESAME
    SEEDS (SEE NOTE)

1 TABLESPOON MINCED FRESH GINGER

1 TABLESPOON RICE WINE VINEGAR

1/2 TEASPOON ASIAN CHILI PASTE

4 LOIN PORK CHOPS, ABOUT 1 1/2
    INCHES THICK

VEGETABLE OIL COOKING SPRAY

1. Combine the soy sauce, scallions, sugar, sesame seeds, ginger, vinegar, and chili paste in a small bowl, stirring well.

2. Put the pork chops in a shallow glass or ceramic dish and pour the marinade over them. Turn to coat. Cover and set aside at room temperature for about 30 minutes, or refrigerate for as long as 8 hours.

3. Prepare a charcoal or gas grill. Lightly spray the grill rack with vegetable oil cooking spray. The coals should be moderately hot.

4. Lift the chops from the marinade, reserving the marinade. Grill for about 10 minutes on each side, turning several times with tongs and brushing 2 or 3 times with the marinade during the first 10 or 15 minutes of cooking. Grill until a meat thermometer inserted in the center of the meatiest sections registers 150° to 155°F. Let the chops rest for a few minutes before serving.

A sweet meat such as pork marries well with sweet ingredients, like the maple syrup found in this marinade. Although we recommend loin chops, rib pork chops work equally well here. You could also marinate blade pork chops, which are cut from the blade roast and are larger and more robust than other pork chops. Grill blade chops a little longer than loin chops.

Maple-Flavored Pork Chops   *Serves 6*

6 LOIN PORK CHOPS, ABOUT 1 1/2
   INCHES THICK
FRESHLY GROUND BLACK PEPPER TO
   TASTE
VEGETABLE OIL COOKING SPRAY
1 1/2 CUPS MAPLE SYRUP MARINADE
   (PAGE 192)

1. Trim the pork chops, if necessary, and rub pepper into both sides of the meat. Put the chops in a shallow glass or ceramic dish and pour the marinade over the meat, turning several times to coat. Cover and refrigerate for at least 4 hours or overnight.

2. Prepare a charcoal or gas grill. Lightly spray the grill rack with vegetable oil cooking spray. The coals should be moderately hot.

3. Lift the chops from the marinade, reserving the marinade. Grill for about 10 minutes on each side, turning several times with tongs and brushing 2 or 3 times with the marinade during the first 10 or 15 minutes of cooking. Grill until a meat thermometer inserted in the center of the meatiest sections registers 150° to 155°F. Let the chops rest for a few minutes before serving.

The most commonly grilled pork chops are loin and rib chops, both tender and delicious. Sirloin pork chops are cut from sirloin roast, which is in front of the butt and has wonderfully tender meat and a small round bone. You could use sirloin pork chops for any of these recipes, although they are harder to find in supermarkets and butcher shops than the other cuts.

Loin Pork Chops in Honey-Orange Marinade   *Serves 6*

JUICE OF 4 ORANGES

3 TABLESPOONS OLIVE OIL

3 TABLESPOONS HONEY

3 TABLESPOONS SNIPPED FRESH
CHIVES

1 LARGE CLOVE GARLIC, CRUSHED

1 TEASPOON FRESHLY GROUND BLACK
PEPPER, OR TO TASTE

SALT TO TASTE

6 LOIN PORK CHOPS, ABOUT 1½
INCHES THICK

VEGETABLE OIL COOKING SPRAY

1. Combine the orange juice, oil, honey, chives, garlic, and pepper in a small bowl. Season with salt, stirring well.

2. Trim the pork chops, if necessary, and put in a shallow glass or ceramic dish. Pour the marinade over the chops, turning them several times to coat. Cover and refrigerate for at least 4 hours or overnight. Turn the chops several times during marinating.

3. Prepare a charcoal or gas grill. Lightly spray the grill rack with vegetable oil cooking spray. The coals should be moderately hot.

4. Lift the chops from the marinade, reserving the marinade. Grill for about 10 minutes on each side, turning several times with tongs and brushing 2 or 3 times with the marinade during the first 10 or 15 minutes of cooking. Grill until a meat thermometer inserted in the center of the meatiest sections registers 150° to 155°F. Let the chops rest for a few minutes before serving.

Pork is not as juicy as some meats, but when cooked in foil packets after being soaked in a robust brine for hours, it is surprisingly moist. Try this with any style of pork chops—loin, rib, blade, or sirloin—although we make it with loin chops most often. We refer to these chops as "farmhouse-style," because curing pork in brine is an old-fashioned method. Here, we use the brine for moisture only—not curing.

Grilled Farmhouse-Style Pork Chops

2 CUPS APPLE CIDER

1/2 CUP FIRMLY PACKED LIGHT OR DARK BROWN SUGAR

1/2 CUP LIGHTLY PACKED FRESH THYME SPRIGS

3 TABLESPOONS SALT

2 TABLESPOONS COARSELY CHOPPED FRESH HOT CHILI OR 1/4 TEASPOON CRUSHED RED PEPPER

12 WHOLE ALLSPICE BERRIES

2 BAY LEAVES

ONE 2-INCH STICK CINNAMON

1 TEASPOON BLACK PEPPERCORNS

6 LOIN PORK CHOPS, ABOUT 1 1/2 INCHES THICK

VEGETABLE OIL COOKING SPRAY

1. In a nonreactive saucepan, combine the cider, sugar, thyme, salt, chili, allspice, bay leaves, cinnamon, and peppercorns and bring to a boil over high heat. Reduce the heat to low and cook for about 20 minutes, or until the flavors blend. Set aside to cool completely.

2. Put the pork chops in a glass or ceramic dish small enough so that when the brine is added, it will cover the meat. Add the brine, tucking the spices and herbs around the meat. Cover and refrigerate for 12 hours.

3. Drain the brine from the meat, reserving the herbs and spices.

4. On a work surface, layer 2 or 3 sheets of heavy-duty foil large enough to wrap 2 or 3 chops and lightly spray the top sheet with vegetable oil cooking spray. Place 2 or 3 chops close together and scatter with some of the reserved herbs and spices. Fold the foil over to cover the chops; double wrap the package with more foil. Repeat for the remaining chops.

5. Prepare a charcoal or gas grill, arranging the coals for indirect cooking. The coals should be moderately hot.

6. Put the foil packages on the grill, seam side up away from the heat. Cover and cook for 35 to 40 minutes, adding fresh coals as necessary to keep the heat constantly at a moderate to moderately hot temperature. Using insulated mitts, open the packages occasionally to make sure the meat is gently simmering in its own juices and not cooking too fast. Halfway through cooking, rotate the packages with a spatula so that the side nearest the most intense heat is turned away from it.

7. Remove from the grill and unwrap the packages carefully, taking care not to get burned by the escaping steam. Lift the chops from the packages with tongs, brushing off the herbs and spices. Place the chops on the grill over the most intense heat and cook for 2 or 3 minutes on each side, or until browned and crisp around the edges. An instant-read thermometer inserted in the center of the meatiest section of a chop should register 150° to 155°F. Let the chops rest for a few minutes before serving.

For kabobs, we think the loin meat is best to use, although you can substitute butt, if necessary. The butt, or shoulder, is the most desirable part of the ham and often is labeled "fresh ham" in supermarkets and some butcher shops. Do not confuse it with Boston butt, which is cut from the upper half of the shoulder—while its meat is tender, it is not as good for kabobs as the other two cuts of pork. While the grapes are good with the pork, for a more traditional kabob you could substitute chunks of fresh pineapple.

Pork and Grape Kabobs with Sweet-Sour Sauce   *Serves 4*

SAUCE

1/2 CUP CIDER VINEGAR

1/4 CUP SUGAR

1 CUP ORANGE JUICE

2 TABLESPOONS LIME JUICE

1 SERRANO CHILI, CHOPPED

1 TABLESPOON CHOPPED FRESH
  LEMONGRASS

KABOBS

2 1/2 POUNDS TRIMMED BONELESS PORK
  LOIN OR BUTT, CUT INTO 1 1/2-INCH
  CUBES

1/2 CUP FINELY CHOPPED ONION

1 SERRANO CHILI, CHOPPED

1 TABLESPOON FINELY CHOPPED FRESH
  LEMONGRASS

1 TEASPOON FRESHLY GROUND BLACK
  PEPPER

1. To prepare the sauce, combine the sugar and vinegar in a saucepan and bring to a simmer over medium heat, stirring often, for 5 or 6 minutes, or until reduced in volume by half. Add the orange juice and lime juice, chili, and lemongrass, and cook for about 10 minutes longer, or until the sauce is slightly syrupy. The sauce can be served warm or at room temperature.

2. To prepare the kabobs, put the pork in a glass or ceramic dish and add the onion, chili, lemongrass, pepper, and turmeric. Using your hands, rub the seasonings into the meat. Add the orange juice, lime juice, soy sauce, and oil and mix well, coating the meat. Cover and refrigerate for at least 4 hours and as long as 12 hours.

3. Prepare a charcoal or gas grill. Lightly spray the grill rack with vegetable oil cooking spray. The coals should be moderately hot.

1/4 TEASPOON TURMERIC

3/4 CUP FRESH ORANGE JUICE

3 TABLESPOONS FRESH LIME JUICE

3 TABLESPOONS SOY SAUCE

3 TABLESPOONS CANOLA OIL

VEGETABLE OIL COOKING SPRAY

32 TO 40 LARGE RED SEEDLESS
   GRAPES

FOUR 12-INCH METAL SKEWERS

4. Thread the pork and grapes onto the skewers, beginning and ending with the meat. Grill for 15 to 20 minutes, turning several times with tongs, until done. Serve with the sauce, reheated if desired.

Pork and fruit are an obvious pairing. Be sure to use tenderloin or ham butt (not Boston butt) for these kabobs so that they cook relatively quickly and evenly.

Grilled Curried Pork Kabobs with Pears   *Serves 6*

2½ POUNDS TRIMMED BONELESS PORK LOIN OR BUTT, CUT INTO ABOUT THIRTY 1½-INCH CUBES

6 TABLESPOONS CURRY PASTE RUB (PAGE 199)

4 FIRM, RIPE PEARS, SUCH AS BARTLETT OR BOSC, CORED AND HALVED LENGTHWISE

VEGETABLE OIL COOKING SPRAY

1 RED BELL PEPPER, CUT INTO 12 CHUNKS, EACH ABOUT 1½ INCHES

1 RED ONION, CUT INTO 12 WEDGES

OLIVE OIL

SIX 12-INCH METAL SKEWERS

1. Put the pork in a glass or ceramic bowl and, using your fingers, rub 4 tablespoons curry paste into the meat. Cover and set aside at room temperature for about 30 minutes or refrigerate for as long as 4 hours.

2. Rub the remaining 2 tablespoons of the curry paste on the pears. Cover and refrigerate until ready to grill.

3. Prepare a charcoal or gas grill. Lightly spray the grill rack with vegetable oil cooking spray. The coals should be moderately hot.

4. Thread the pork, peppers, and onions onto skewers, beginning and ending with the meat. Brush or drizzle the meat, vegetables, and the halved pears lightly with olive oil. Place the skewers and pears on the grill and cook, covered, for 12 to 15 minutes, turning frequently with tongs until done. The pears will brown. If the pears seem to be cooking more quickly than the meat, move the skewers to the edge of the grill.

We cook these pork kabobs long and slow over a relatively moderate fire in an effort to approximate the true flavor of Jamaican jerk pork. Buy pork loin or butt with visible fat for this recipe so that it can withstand the long cooking time.

Jerk Pork Kabobs   *Serves 6 to 8*

2½ POUNDS TRIMMED BONELESS PORK
    LOIN OR BUTT, CUT INTO 1½-INCH
    CUBES
¾ CUP JERK SEASONING (PAGE 196)
VEGETABLE OIL COOKING SPRAY
SIX TO EIGHT 12-INCH METAL
    SKEWERS

1. Put the pork in a glass or ceramic bowl and, using your fingers, rub the seasoning into the meat. Cover and refrigerate for at least 4 hours or overnight.

2. Prepare a charcoal or gas grill, arranging the coals for indirect cooking. Lightly spray the grill rack with vegetable oil cooking spray. The coals should be moderately hot.

3. Thread the pork onto six to eight skewers and grill over the hottest part of the fire for about 10 minutes, turning often, until lightly browned. Move the skewers to the cooler part of the grill, cover, and cook for 25 to 30 minutes longer, turning several times, until the pork is very tender.

A pig roast is the ultimate outdoor party, and if you have a large enough grill, you might want to try one. The meat is indescribably tender and tasty and needs no sauce or salsa. It tastes great served with classic summer side dishes, such as coleslaw and potato salad.

You will need a grill that is at least twenty-six to thirty inches long. (A standard round Weber kettle grill is too small.) Buy the largest disposable foil turkey pan, and even so, you may have to bend the sides outward to fit the pig inside. A small pig, such as the one we grill for this recipe, is hard to find. You will have to order it well in advance and may have to locate a specialty butcher. Much more common are larger pigs, weighing about twenty-five pounds. These are too large for a grill—they are cooked in pits. Be sure the butcher cleans and dresses the pig for you, which means it should be free of hair and its eyes should be removed, leaving behind only clean cavities. The intestines and other organs should be cleaned from the beast, and the belly should be split. The pig will have its head, tail, and feet still intact. Wrap the snout, ears, tail, and feet in foil to prevent burning, and even so, do not be surprised if the tail and feet break off during cooking. Very likely, the pig will be frozen when you get it. Let it thaw for about twenty-four hours in the refrigerator before marinating it.

For this recipe, we prepared a typical Italian-style marinade. You can substitute rosemary or tarragon for the thyme, or devise a spicier, Southwestern-style marinade. If you want to add authenticity to the recipe, toss some soaked oak wood chips on the coals to impart a little flavor. Keep the fire relatively cool, and if your grill is not fitted with an external thermometer, use an oven thermometer to determine its temperature, which should be about 325°F. Gas grills are far easier to control when grilling a pig, but you can have great success with a charcoal fire, too.

A small, fifteen-pound pig needs only ten minutes to the pound to cook because the meat-to-bone ratio is relatively low. However, if you attempt to pit-roast a larger pig, the time will go up to at least twenty minutes a pound. But that is for another book!

Grilled Suckling Pig   *Serves 10 to 14*

1 CUP OLIVE OIL

JUICE OF 3 LEMONS

3 CLOVES GARLIC, CHOPPED

2 TABLESPOONS CHOPPED FRESH
   THYME

1. Combine the olive oil, lemon juice, garlic, thyme, parsley, and fennel seeds in a bowl. Season generously with pepper, stirring well.

2 TABLESPOONS CHOPPED FRESH FLAT-
   LEAF PARSLEY
1 TEASPOON CRUSHED FENNEL SEEDS
FRESHLY GROUND BLACK PEPPER TO
   TASTE
ONE 15-POUND SUCKLING PIG,
   CLEANED AND DRESSED
ABOUT 3 CUPS WHITE WINE
ABOUT 3 CUPS CHICKEN BROTH

2. Using your hands, rub the pig with the marinade, inside and out, working it into the meat. Transfer the pig to a large plastic bag (such as a garbage bag), pour any remaining marinade over the pig, and seal the bag. Put this bag inside another bag (the first bag will be greasy) and fold closed. Refrigerate for at least 8 hours, or overnight. Let the pig come to room temperature at least 1 hour before grilling.

3. Prepare a charcoal or gas grill; if the grill is large enough, prepare it for indirect grilling. The coals should be moderately hot. During grilling, the internal temperature of the grill should be maintained at 325°F.

4. Wrap the pig's tail, feet, ears and snout with foil to prevent burning. Put a metal roasting rack in the largest size foil turkey pan. Set the pig on its back on the rack. Pour enough wine and broth into the pan to reach a depth of 1 to 2 inches. If using the indirect grilling method, set the pan over the cooler part of the grill.

5. Grill the pig in the pan, with the grill covered, for about 3 hours (10 minutes to the pound). Baste the pig often (every 15 or 20 minutes) with the pan drippings, turning it several times for even browning. Add more wine, broth, or water (or a mixture of all three) to the pan as necessary. The pig should begin and end grilling on its back. The pig is done when the internal temperature of the thickest section, the rump, reaches 150°F. The thickest part will reach 160°F during resting.

6. Let the pig rest for at least 30 minutes before serving. Transfer the pig to a large cutting board. Remove the head and legs. Slice the meat from the legs, as you would from a turkey drumstick. Peel the skin from the body, using your fingers and a sharp knife. Remove the thick layer of fat just beneath the skin. Carve the meat from the bones, slicing it diagonally, working forward towards the head end. When you have cut as much meat as possible this way, tear the rib cage apart into ribs and slice what meat there is from the ribs. Serve immediately.

CHAPTER 5

POULTRY

Grilled chicken is fast becoming as popular as grilled burgers or steaks in America's backyards—and in some households it is a far more familiar sight on the grill than red meat. Chicken and turkey, both well suited for the grill as are other types of poultry, are widely available, are relatively inexpensive, and because of their mildness, lend themselves to both subtle and bold flavorings in the guises of marinades, rubs, and pastes. Plus, as we all know, poultry—and white meat in particular—is especially heart and health friendly. Who can argue with such merits? Not us, nor would we want to. We love grilled poultry!

We wish everyone would buy poultry from reputable butchers, who usually have the best birds. However, most folks rely on supermarkets for chicken and other poultry, usually because these all-purpose markets are their only choice but also because they are convenient. If they shop at a butcher at all, most home cooks reserve the trip for more expensive meats, which is too bad. As with all meat and poultry purchases, establishing a relationship with your butcher can make a big difference in quality and service.

When buying poultry, buy Grade A, which is roughly equivalent to prime meat (however, Grades B and C poultry rarely are available to retail consumers). For chicken, look for even coloring that is neither bright yellow nor dead white. The chicken should be slightly yellow, which is a sure sign that the bird was fed corn. The birds should be plump, with well-developed breasts and rounded thighs, both of which indicate firm meat and a good inner coating of fat. Avoid chickens that appear scrawny or dried up. It's always a good idea to buy whole chickens and cut them up yourself because the less the chicken has been handled, the better, and this will save money. Avoid chicken in packages where you can see puddles of water, which could mean that the bird has been frozen, thawed, and refrozen—a process that will leave the meat chewy and dry.

Turkeys should be pale colored and some even have a bluish cast, which is perfectly acceptable. Their breasts should be plump and nicely formed and the thighs rounded. Buy only fresh turkeys; frozen birds are tasteless and dry. Rock Cornish game hens, the third type of poultry we address in this chapter, should be plump and pale colored.

Many chefs recommend buying free-range chickens and other poultry. At the very least, the consumer is regularly advised to buy "minimally processed" chicken. We don't disagree with this advice, but we are not sure either term means much. Free-range poultry should refer to birds that are raised in natural surroundings where they can peck and scratch in the dirt for organically grown feed under the shining sun. Minimally processed, on the other hand, should refer to birds that are not overmedicated when alive or treated with unnecessary chemicals after slaughter. However, neither term is universally trustworthy. Instead, we suggest buying chickens and other poultry that at the very least have labels reading "no antibiotics administered" or "no animal byproducts in feed," or both. If your butcher stands behind his free-range poultry, which ideally means he knows the farmers who supply him, then buy these birds, despite their higher cost. They will be tastier and tenderer, and less fatty than others.

Grilling can be kind to poultry, whether it's chicken, Rock Cornish game hens, turkey, duck, quail, or pheasant. (In this chapter, we address only the first three birds, dealing with the others in our chapter on game on page 155.) The birds pick up just enough of the charred flavor to be deliciously appealing and they mark nicely with seared lines when laid on a hot grill rack. But without proper tending, the kindness sours. The poultry runs the risk of burning and drying out near the surface while staying uncooked at the bone. To avoid this, turn the birds during grilling: stand at the grill and use long-handled tongs to turn the poultry pieces often. This will encourage even cooking without burning. Even whole chickens roasted on the grill should be turned several times. Whole turkeys, however, do not require turning.

As with all grilling, use our cooking times as guides—not absolutes. Every grill and every fire burns somewhat differently and therefore the poultry may cook faster or slower than the recipe indicates. Get to know your own grill and your grilling style, and you will soon understand how it cooks.

In addition, rely on a meat thermometer—nothing is less appetizing than undercooked poultry and, frankly, it is not safe to eat. Dark meat in both chicken and turkey should be cooked to an internal temperature of 180° to 185°F, and white meat to 170°F. When using a thermometer, insert it in the thickest section of meat and don't let it touch the bone.

Preparing Poultry for Grilling

Poultry should be cooked soon after purchase and should never be left at room temperature longer than necessary. Do not unwrap it, but store it in its original packaging in the coldest part of the refrigerator, which usually is the rear of the lowest shelf.

When you are ready to prepare the poultry, take it from the refrigerator and let it come to room temperature, which means leaving it on the counter for about 30 minutes. If it is a particularly hot, humid summer day, reduce this time by up to 10 minutes. Pat the chicken or turkey dry with paper towels and then either marinate it, rub it with dry rub, or otherwise prepare it for the grill. We have not included the important step of drying the meat in the recipe instructions, because it is universally appropriate for all recipes calling for beef, veal, poultry, lamb, or pork. As soon as the chicken or other poultry is seasoned, return it to the refrigerator until you are ready to cook.

Although we have recipes for whole chicken, we also have recipes that call for chickens cut into eight pieces. These pieces represent the breast halves, thighs, legs, and wings. Most chicken producers pack chicken cut into these pieces, but it is not difficult to cut whole chickens into these parts; discard the back or use it for making stock. And of course you can ask the butcher to cut the chicken for you.

Raw poultry runs the risk of carrying harmful bacteria, regardless of the brand, quality, or source. Cooking it renders it not only harmless but also healthful and delicious. However, when working with the raw birds, exercise sensible caution. Wash all work surfaces with warm, soapy water; keep other foods away from the birds and their juices; and be sure to wash your hands and cooking tools before moving on to your next culinary task.

Boneless or Bone-In Chicken on the Grill

Recipes for bone-in chicken parts can be made with boneless, skinless chicken breasts, and vice versa. For a recipe that serves six, you will need two whole chickens (each weighing about three pounds) cut into eight pieces. For the same recipe, you will need two to two and one-quarter pounds of boneless, skinless chicken breast meat, although it's more important to have at least six boneless chicken breast halves for easy serving.

To convert a recipe for boneless, skinless chicken breasts to bone-in chicken parts, grill the chicken for forty to forty-five minutes altogether, beginning with the legs and thighs, which will need about fifteen minutes on the grill before the white meat breasts are laid on the grill. To prevent burning, start the chicken with the skin side up and while the chicken parts should be turned frequently during grilling, they should spend more time with the skin sides up than down. The chicken is done when the juices run clear when the thickest sections of the meat are pierced with a fork or sharp knife. You can also insert a meat thermometer into the dark meat to make sure it registers 180°F, or into the white meat for 170°F. Be sure the thermometer does not touch the bone.

To convert a recipe for bone-in chicken to one for boneless breasts, cook the breasts for twelve to sixteen minutes, turning them several times, until they are cooked through.

Practical Freezing

We prefer to grill meat and poultry fresh, but we appreciate the fact that it freezes well, which is a practical consideration for many people. Although we never sell meat that has been frozen, we are well aware that our customers often freeze the meat we sell—and because we want them to enjoy their purchase, regardless of whether they eat it right away or freeze it, we have some suggestions for successful freezing.

If you plan to freeze meat or poultry, do so as soon as you get home. If it's wrapped in supermarket plastic, leave it in the original packaging. The same goes for butcher paper. Wrap another layer of sturdy plastic wrap around the package, making sure it is well protected. Do not use foil for overwrapping, because it becomes brittle in the freezer and can rip. Put the package inside a heavy, freezer-quality plastic bag with a zipped closure, making sure the bag is large enough to hold the meat comfortably. Press as much air from the bag as you can before sealing it so that it collapses around the meat. Clearly mark the bag, making sure to date it. Stash the bag in the far reaches of the freezer, which is the coldest part. When it is frozen solid, you can shift it around to make room for other foods.

If you are concerned that your freezer may not be cold enough for meat, consider this: If it is cold enough to freeze ice cream hard, it is cold enough to freeze meat and poultry. But even having the coldest freezer does not mean you can leave the meat in it indefinitely. For the best texture and quality, do not leave meat in the deep freeze for longer than 30 days in the winter, or 15 days in the summer.

Let meat thaw slowly in the refrigerator. This can take from one to two days, depending on the time of year and the size and cut of the meat. If you are planning to slice the meat for kabobs or stew, keep in mind that it is easier to slice when partially frozen.

Even with careful wrapping, sometimes food develops freezer burn. We don't advise grilling the damaged meat, but don't discard it, either. Cut it up and stew or braise it.

How to Guarantee Juicy and Moist Boneless, Skinless Chicken Breasts

Although we do not insist that you take this extra step (you won't find it in the recipes), we have found that boneless, skinless chicken breasts remain moister and juicier if you precook them before marinating and grilling. To do so, bring an inch or so of water to a boil in a deep skillet and poach the chicken breasts for one minute—this will not cook them through but will give them a head start. Remove them from the water, cool for a few minutes, and then marinate them or otherwise prepare them for grilling. Even when refrigerated for several hours after poaching, the chicken breasts will be plumper and juicier than otherwise.

If you come across boneless chicken breasts with the skin on, buy them. The skin adds great flavor and moisture. Begin grilling with the skin side up to prevent burning. The skin will crisp when you turn the breasts.

Leftover Strategy

Who doesn't love leftovers? Especially grilled leftovers? The charred flavor remains with the meat or poultry, making it nearly as enticing the next day as it was right off the grill. For this reason, cook extra when you can. You will never regret it.

As soon as you realize you will have some leftovers, put the food away in the refrigerator. It is never a good idea to leave any food, even cooked food, at room temperature for more than an hour, and this is particularly true in the hot summer months when we tend to fire up the grill more often. Room temperatures are the most dangerous for food because it is at these temperatures that bacteria thrive. Wrap the leftovers well in plastic or put them in rigid plastic storage containers with fitted lids. Eat them within a day or two, at the most.

If you want to reheat the leftover meat, wrap it in foil and put it on the grill. The coals should be arranged for indirect cooking and they should be only moderately hot. However, most grilled meat and poultry tastes terrific cold. Slice it for sandwiches or salads.

This and the following five recipes are for chickens cut into parts, which is how many people prefer grilled chicken—it's easy to serve and to eat.

Lobel's Herbed Grilled Chicken

Serves 6 to 8

1 CUP CANOLA OIL

2 TABLESPOONS DRIED ITALIAN
   SEASONING

1 TEASPOON DRIED BASIL

1 TEASPOON DRIED OREGANO

2 LARGE CLOVES GARLIC, MINCED

6 TABLESPOONS PREPARED MUSTARD

TWO 3- TO 3½-POUND CHICKENS,
   EACH CUT INTO 8 PIECES

SALT TO TASTE

VEGETABLE OIL COOKING SPRAY

1. Combine the oil, seasoning, basil, oregano, garlic, and mustard in a small bowl, whisking until smooth.

2. Sprinkle the chicken with salt and put the pieces in a large glass or ceramic dish. Pour the marinade over the chicken and toss to coat. Cover and refrigerate for at least 1 hour and as long as 6 hours.

3. Prepare a charcoal or gas grill. Lightly spray the grill rack with vegetable oil cooking spray. The coals should be moderately hot.

4. Lift the chicken from the marinade, reserving the marinade. Grill the legs and thighs, skin side up to start, for about 15 minutes, turning with tongs frequently and brushing several times with the marinade. Place the breasts and wings on the grill, skin side up to start. Cook all the chicken for 25 to 30 minutes longer, turning often and brushing several times with marinade during the first 10 minutes of cooking. The chicken is done when the juices run clear when the thickest sections are pierced with a fork or sharp knife, or when an instant-read thermometer inserted into the thickest part of the thigh registers 180°F and the thickest part of the breast registers 170°F. Don't let the thermometer touch the bone. Serve immediately.

Bacon-Mushroom Burger

Grilled Sirloin Steak with Green Chili Sauce

Sirloin Steak Kabobs with Rosemary-Brushed Potatoes and Red Peppers

Tortilla-Wrapped Round Steak

Lamb Chops with Grilled Stuffed Mushrooms

Southwest-Style Pork Chops with Ancho Chili Powder

Grilled Chicken Breasts and Apple Rings with Maple Syrup Marinade

Grilled Quail with Raspberry-Cranberry Cumberland Sauce

The chickens in markets are labeled as broilers, fryers, roasters, and broiler-fryers. Unfortunately, these monikers can be inconsistent. For these recipes we recommend roasters (at times also called "pullets"), which have more meat than broiler-fryers. However, broiler-fryers are acceptable choices, too. As a rule, fryers and broilers are smaller than roasters and broiler-fryers.

Fired-Up Chipotle Chicken
Serves 6 to 8

4 CLOVES GARLIC

3 CHIPOTLE CHILIES IN ADOBO SAUCE
   (SEE NOTE)

1/4 CUP RED WINE VINEGAR

2 TEASPOONS SALT

JUICE OF 1 LEMON

GRATED ZEST OF 1 LEMON

TWO 3- TO 3 1/2-POUND CHICKENS,
   EACH CUT INTO 8 PIECES

VEGETABLE OIL COOKING SPRAY

1. Combine the garlic, chilies, vinegar, salt, lemon juice, and lemon zest in a food processor and pulse 4 or 5 times to make a paste.

2. Put the chicken pieces in a glass or ceramic dish and rub the paste thoroughly into the meat. Cover and refrigerate for at least 3 hours or overnight.

3. Prepare a charcoal or gas grill. Lightly spray the grill rack with vegetable oil cooking spray. The coals should be moderately hot.

4. Lift the chicken from the marinade, reserving the marinade. Grill the legs and thighs, skin side up to start, for about 15 minutes, turning with tongs frequently and brushing several times with the marinade. Place the breasts and wings on the grill, skin side up to start. Cook all the chicken for 25 to 30 minutes longer, turning often and brushing several times with marinade during the first 10 minutes of cooking. The chicken is done when the juices run clear when the thickest sections are pierced with a fork or sharp knife, or when an instant-read thermometer inserted into the thickest part of the thigh registers 180°F and the thickest part of the breast registers 170°F. Don't let the thermometer touch the bone. Serve immediately.

note: When rubbing the chicken with the paste, wear plastic gloves to protect your hands. If you have no gloves, wash your hands as soon as you are finished.

Whether you use a roaster or boiler-fryer, be sure to rub the spice mixture well into the meat. As it marinates, the dry rub will coax the natural juices to the surface of the meat and the chicken will marinate. This works for other meats, too, such as pork and beef.

Spicy-Rubbed Chicken   *Serves 6 to 8*

TWO 3- TO 3½-POUND CHICKENS,
EACH CUT INTO 8 PIECES
3 TABLESPOONS SPICY DRY RUB
(PAGE 194)
VEGETABLE OIL COOKING SPRAY
MADISON AVENUE BARBECUE SAUCE
(PAGE 173)

1. Put the chicken pieces in a glass or ceramic dish and rub the seasoning thoroughly into the meat. Cover and refrigerate for 6 to 8 hours.

2. Prepare a charcoal or gas grill. Lightly spray the grill rack with vegetable oil cooking spray. The coals should be moderately hot.

3. Grill the legs and thighs, skin side up to start, for about 15 minutes, turning with tongs frequently. Place the breasts and wings on the grill, skin side up to start. Cook all the chicken for 25 to 30 minutes longer, turning often. The chicken is done when the juices run clear when the thickest sections are pierced with a fork or sharp knife, or when an instant-read thermometer inserted into the thickest part of the thigh registers 180°F and the thickest part of the breast registers 170°F. Don't let the thermometer touch the bone. Serve immediately with the barbecue sauce.

ever buy chicken parts that are bruised or discolored, but instead look for even, yellowish coloration and plump breasts and thighs. This marinade, redolent with the flavors of Asia, blends beautifully with the chicken, although it would taste good, too, with pork.

Gingery Chicken   *Serves 6 to 8*

½ CUP SOY SAUCE

¼ CUP RICE WINE VINEGAR

3 TABLESPOONS FRESH LEMON JUICE

1 TABLESPOON HONEY

1½ TABLESPOONS CHOPPED FRESH
     GINGER

1 CLOVE GARLIC, CHOPPED

½ TEASPOON CRUSHED RED PEPPER

SALT AND FRESHLY GROUND BLACK
     PEPPER TO TASTE

TWO 3- TO 3½-POUND CHICKENS,
     EACH CUT INTO EIGHT PIECES

VEGETABLE OIL COOKING SPRAY

1. Combine the soy sauce, vinegar, lemon juice, honey, ginger, garlic, and crushed red pepper in a nonreactive saucepan. Season with salt and pepper. Bring to a boil, remove from the heat, and let cool.

2. Transfer the marinade to a shallow glass or ceramic dish and add the chicken pieces. Turn several times to coat. Cover and refrigerate for 4 to 6 hours.

3. Prepare a charcoal or gas grill. Lightly spray the grill rack with vegetable oil cooking spray. The coals should be moderately hot.

4. Lift the chicken from the marinade, reserving the marinade. Grill the legs and thighs, skin side up to start, for about 15 minutes, turning with tongs frequently and brushing several times with the marinade. Place the breasts and wings on the grill, skin side up to start. Cook all the chicken for 25 to 30 minutes longer, turning often and brushing several times with marinade during the first 10 minutes of cooking. The chicken is done when the juices run clear when the thickest sections are pierced with a fork or sharp knife, or when an instant-read thermometer inserted into the thickest part of the thigh registers 180°F and the thickest part of the breast registers 170°F. Don't let the thermometer touch the bone. Serve immediately.

In this recipe, we skin the chicken and then rub the spice mixture deep into the meat. This method flavors the meat more intensely than if it were protected by the chicken skin. The cool chutney offsets the curry flavor.

Curried Chicken with Mango-Curry Chutney
Serves 6

TWO 3- TO 3½-POUND CHICKENS, EACH CUT INTO EIGHT PIECES AND SKINNED

¾ CUP CURRY PASTE RUB (PAGE 199)

1 TABLESPOON CANOLA OR SAFFLOWER OIL

3 TABLESPOONS CHOPPED ONIONS

1 SMALL SERRANO CHILI, CHOPPED

1 MANGO, PEELED, CORED, AND CUBED (SEE NOTE)

2 TABLESPOONS FRESH ORANGE JUICE

1 TEASPOON CIDER VINEGAR

FRESHLY GROUND BLACK PEPPER TO TASTE

2 TABLESPOONS CHOPPED CILANTRO

VEGETABLE OIL COOKING SPRAY

1. Put the chicken pieces in a glass or ceramic dish and rub all but 1 tablespoon of the curry rub thoroughly into the meat. Cover and refrigerate for at least 30 minutes and as long as 4 hours.

2. Heat the oil in a small skillet over medium heat. Add the onions and cook for 3 or 4 minutes, or until the onions begin to soften. Add the chilies and cook for about 30 seconds, just until fragrant. Add the mango, orange juice, vinegar, and the remaining tablespoon of curry rub and cook, stirring occasionally, for 5 to 7 minutes, or until the mango softens but still retains its shape. Season with pepper to taste and stir in the cilantro. Cook for about 1 minute longer and transfer to a bowl. Cover and refrigerate until chilled. (The chutney will keep for up to 3 days.)

3. Prepare a charcoal or gas grill. Lightly spray the grill rack with vegetable oil cooking spray. The coals should be moderately hot.

4. Grill the legs and thighs, skin side up to start, for about 15 minutes, turning with tongs frequently. Place the breasts and wings on the grill, skin side up to start. Cook all the chicken for 25 to 30 minutes longer, turning often. The chicken is done when the juices run clear when the thickest sections are pierced with a fork or sharp knife, or when an instant-read thermometer inserted into the thickest part of the thigh registers 180°F and the thickest part of the breast registers 170°F. Don't let the thermometer touch the bone. Serve immediately with the chutney.

note: It's important to use perfectly ripe fruit. A ripe mango feels soft when gently pressed, much like a ripe avocado or peach. Depending on the variety, mangoes may be difficult to cube, because the fruit may be very soft and juicy when ripe. To make it easy, hold the mango on its side and cut straight down along the edge of the large, center seed. Cut along the opposite side of the seed in the same way. With the fruit still attached to the skin, score it into cubes, and then turn the skin inside out, making it easy to slice the cubes from the skin. Slice the remaining fruit clinging to the seed and add it to the chutney.

Teriyaki chicken is a backyard classic. This marinade is great on chicken, but also good with beef or pork.

Teriyaki Chicken   *Serves 6*

TWO 3- TO 3½-POUND CHICKENS,
EACH CUT INTO 8 PIECES
2 CUPS TERIYAKI MARINADE (PAGE 191)
VEGETABLE OIL COOKING SPRAY

1. Put the chicken in a glass or ceramic dish and pour the marinade over the chicken pieces, turning the chicken to coat. Cover and refrigerate for at least 2 hours and as long as 24 hours.

2. Prepare a charcoal or gas grill. Lightly spray the grill rack with vegetable oil cooking spray. The coals should be moderately hot

3. Lift the chicken from the marinade, reserving the marinade. Grill the legs and thighs, skin side up to start, for about 15 minutes, turning with tongs frequently and brushing several times with the marinade. Place the breasts and wings on the grill, skin side up to start. Cook all the chicken for 25 to 30 minutes longer, turning often and brushing several times with marinade during the first 10 minutes of cooking. The chicken is done when the juices run clear when the thickest sections are pierced with a fork or sharp knife, or when an instant-read thermometer inserted into the thickest part of the thigh registers 180°F and the thickest part of the breast registers 170°F. Don't let the thermometer touch the bone. Serve immediately.

The mild, sweet flavor of chicken makes it a natural to pair with fruit, particularly when the chicken has been soaked in a slightly sweet marinade. Try this with pork, too.

Grilled Chicken Breasts and Apple Rings with Maple Syrup Marinade

Serves 6

6 BONE-IN CHICKEN BREAST HALVES

1½ CUPS MAPLE SYRUP MARINADE
(PAGE 192)

VEGETABLE OIL COOKING SPRAY

3 LARGE FIRM APPLES, SUCH AS
CORTLAND OR GRANNY SMITH,
CORED, PEELED AND CUT INTO
1-INCH-THICK RINGS

CANOLA OIL FOR BRUSHING

1. Put the chicken breasts in a shallow glass or ceramic dish. Pour 1¼ cups of the marinade over the chicken, turning to coat. Cover and refrigerate for at least 4 hours and as long as 24 hours. Refrigerate the remaining ¼ cup of marinade.

2. Prepare a charcoal or gas grill. Lightly spray the grill rack with vegetable oil cooking spray. The coals should be moderately hot.

3. Put the apple rings on a plate or baking sheet and brush on both sides with the remaining ¼ cup marinade. Set aside at room temperature to marinate while grilling the chicken.

4. Lift the chicken from the marinade, reserving the marinade. Grill the chicken breasts skin side down, for 25 to 30 minutes, turning with tongs frequently and brushing several times with any remaining marinade during the first 10 minutes of cooking. During the last 10 minutes of grilling, place the apples rings on the outer edge of the grill. Brush with some oil and grill for about 5 minutes. Turn, brush with some more oil and grill for about 5 minutes longer, or until lightly browned on both sides and tender.

5. The chicken is done when the juices run clear when the thickest sections are pierced with a fork, or when an instant-read thermometer (don't touch the bone) inserted into the thickest part of the breast registers 170°F. Serve immediately with the apple slices.

Although you could use this marinade on a whole chicken with both white and dark meat, it is pungent enough to stand up to dark meat alone. Look for plump thighs with no drying or wrinkling on the skin.

Curried Chicken Thighs   *Serves 6*

½ CUP FRESH ORANGE JUICE

3 TABLESPOONS MILD OR HOT INDIAN CURRY PASTE, DEPENDING ON PREFERENCE (SEE NOTE)

2 TABLESPOONS HONEY MUSTARD

2 TEASPOONS SALT

½ TEASPOON GROUND ALLSPICE

½ TEASPOON FRESHLY GROUND BLACK PEPPER

4½ TO 5 POUNDS CHICKEN THIGHS (ABOUT 12 PIECES)

VEGETABLE OIL COOKING SPRAY

1. Combine the orange juice, curry paste, mustard, salt, allspice, and pepper in a glass or ceramic bowl, stirring well to dissolve the paste and mustard completely.

2. Trim the chicken of excess fat and skin, but do not remove most of the skin. Put the thighs in a shallow glass or ceramic dish and rub the paste into the meat, being sure to coat well and to rub some paste under the chicken skin. Cover and refrigerate for at least 2 hours or overnight.

3. Prepare a charcoal or gas grill. Lightly spray the grill rack with vegetable oil cooking spray. The coals should be moderately hot.

4. Grill the chicken thighs for 40 to 45 minutes, turning often with tongs. The chicken is done when the juices run clear when pierced with a fork or sharp knife, or when an instant-read thermometer registers 180°F when inserted in the thickest part of the thighs. Don't let the thermometer touch the bone. Serve immediately.

note: Indian curry paste is sold in small tubs in Asian markets as well as in some supermarkets and specialty food stores. Select hot or mild paste, depending on personal preference.

Everyone seems to love chicken wings—they're easy to eat with your fingers, are inexpensive, and can be served as a snack or as part of the main meal.

Grilled Chicken Wings with Lime Vinaigrette
Serves 6

VEGETABLE OIL COOKING SPRAY

20 TO 25 CHICKEN WINGS

1 TABLESPOON CAYENNE PEPPER

SALT AND FRESHLY GROUND BLACK
   PEPPER TO TASTE

3/4 CUP OLIVE OIL

6 TABLESPOONS FRESH LIME JUICE

4 CLOVES GARLIC, CHOPPED

3/4 CUP CHOPPED FLAT-LEAF PARSLEY

1. Prepare a charcoal or gas grill. Lightly spray the grill rack with vegetable oil cooking spray. The coals should be moderately hot.

2. Prepare the wings by cutting through the joint to make 2 pieces. Snip off the tips. Spread the wings on a baking pan and sprinkle with cayenne, salt, and pepper. Turn and season the other side of the wings. Rub the seasoning into the wings, if necessary, to coat the wings evenly.

3. Combine the olive oil, lime juice, garlic, and parsley in a small glass or ceramic bowl. Season with salt and pepper, stirring well. Set aside.

4. Grill the wings, turning with tongs 3 or 4 times, for 25 to 30 minutes until cooked through. Remove the wings from the grill and transfer to a shallow dish. Whisk the vinaigrette and pour over the wings, tossing to coat. Serve immediately.

When preparing chicken wings for the grill, we suggest snipping off the tips. The wings look better—and no one eats the tips anyway.

Peppery Chicken Wings   *Serves 6*

20 TO 25 CHICKEN WINGS

3 TABLESPOONS PEPPERY DRY RUB

   (PAGE 193)

VEGETABLE OIL COOKING SPRAY

1. Prepare the wings by cutting through the joint to make 2 pieces. Snip off the tips. Spread the wings on a baking pan and sprinkle with half the dry rub. Turn and season the other side of the wings. Rub the seasoning into the wings, if necessary, to coat the wings evenly. Cover and refrigerate for at least 1 hour or overnight.

2. Prepare a charcoal or gas grill. Lightly spray the grill rack with vegetable oil cooking spray. The coals should be moderately hot.

3. Grill the wings, turning with tongs 3 or 4 times, for 25 to 30 minutes until cooked through. Serve immediately.

Try this sweet-and-sour glaze on other chicken parts, but we find it especially tasty on tiny wings to serve with ice cold beer or soda for a casual backyard gathering.

Glazed Sweet-and-Sour Chicken Wings   *Serves 6*

20 TO 25 CHICKEN WINGS

¼ CUP HOISIN SAUCE

1½ TABLESPOONS SOY SAUCE

1 TABLESPOON CATSUP

1 TABLESPOON RICE WINE VINEGAR

1 TABLESPOON FRESH LIME JUICE

1 TEASPOON BROWN SUGAR

1 TEASPOON CHOPPED GARLIC

1 TEASPOON CHOPPED FRESH GINGER

¼ TEASPOON ASIAN CHILI PASTE

VEGETABLE OIL COOKING SPRAY

1. Prepare the wings by cutting through the joint to make 2 pieces. Snip off the tips. Put the wings in a shallow glass or ceramic dish.

2. Combine the hoisin sauce, soy sauce, catsup, vinegar, lime juice, sugar, garlic, ginger, and chili paste in a small bowl and whisk well. Brush liberally on the chicken wings, turning them to coat both sides. Cover and refrigerate for at least 1 hour or overnight.

3. Prepare a charcoal or gas grill. Lightly spray the grill rack with vegetable oil cooking spray. The coals should be moderately hot.

4. Grill the wings, turning with tongs 3 or 4 times and brushing with any remaining glaze during the first 10 minutes of grilling, for 25 to 30 minutes, or until cooked through. Serve immediately.

Splitting chickens down the backbone enables you to lay them flat on the grill. Ask the butcher to butterfly the chicken for you, or simply press the chicken as flat as you can using your hand.

Southeast Asian Ginger-Lemongrass Chicken *Serves 6*

½ CUP PEANUT OIL

JUICE OF 2 LEMONS

1 CUP CHOPPED CILANTRO

1 CUP CHOPPED SCALLIONS (7 OR 8 SCALLIONS)

2 CLOVES GARLIC, CHOPPED

2 TABLESPOONS CHOPPED FRESH GINGER

4 OR 5 STALKS LEMONGRASS, CHOPPED

GRATED ZEST OF 1 LEMON

TWO 2½- TO 3-POUND CHICKENS, SPLIT

VEGETABLE OIL COOKING SPRAY

1. Combine the oil, lemon juice, cilantro, scallions, garlic, ginger, lemongrass, and lemon zest in a bowl.

2. Using a small knife, loosen the chicken skin. Put the chickens in a shallow glass or ceramic dish and pour the marinade over them. Using a spoon or your fingers, push some cilantro, scallions, garlic, ginger, and lemongrass underneath the loosened skin. Turn to coat, cover, and refrigerate for 4 to 6 hours.

3. Prepare a charcoal or gas grill. Lightly spray the grill rack with vegetable oil cooking spray. The coals should be moderately hot.

4. Grill the chicken, skin side up to start, for 30 to 40 minutes, turning several times. Cook until the juices run clear when the thigh meat is pierced with a fork or sharp knife, or an instant-read thermometer inserted in the thickest part of the thigh registers 180°F. Don't let the thermometer touch the bone. Serve.

When roasting a whole chicken on the grill, begin with a plump roaster or broiler-fryer. You can also roast capons on the grill, which are fat, compact male birds that are castrated at an early age to promote plumpness, tenderness, and sweet flavor.

Mahogany-Glazed Chicken   *Serves 6 to 8*

1½ CUPS DARK BEER (SEE NOTE)

½ CUP WORCESTERSHIRE SAUCE

1 ONION, SLICED VERY THIN

1 TABLESPOON DIJON MUSTARD

1 TABLESPOON SALT

2 TEASPOONS SWEET PAPRIKA

TWO 3- TO 3½-POUND CHICKENS

VEGETABLE OIL COOKING SPRAY

1 TABLESPOON MOLASSES

1. Combine the beer, Worcestershire sauce, onion, mustard, salt, and paprika in a small bowl, stirring well.

2. Put the chickens, breast side down, in a shallow glass or ceramic dish and pour the marinade over them. Cover and refrigerate for 4 hours or overnight.

3. Prepare a charcoal or gas grill, arranging the coals for indirect cooking or lighting one side of the grill. Lightly spray the grill rack with vegetable oil cooking spray. The coals should be moderately hot.

4. Lift the chicken from the marinade. Transfer the marinade to a small saucepan. Place the chickens over the cooler part of the grill, cover, and cook for 1 hour and 20 minutes to 1 hour and 30 minutes, or until the juices run clear when the thigh meat is pierced with a fork or sharp knife. An instant-read thermometer inserted in the thickest part of the thigh should register 180°F. Don't let the thermometer touch the bone. Add fresh coals to the fire as necessary to maintain a moderate, constant heat. If using a gas grill, adjust the burner furthest from the chicken to medium. Turn the chicken with tongs 3 or 4 times during grilling to brown evenly on all sides.

5. Meanwhile, bring the marinade to a boil over medium-high heat. Reduce the heat and simmer for about 20 minutes until reduced to about 1 cup. Add the molasses, stir, and cook for 5 minutes longer. Remove ¼ cup of the marinade and set aside the rest.

6. During the final 5 minutes of grilling, brush the chicken with the $1/4$ cup of marinade, turning the chicken to crisp the skin on all sides. Let the chickens sit for at least 10 minutes for the juices to collect. Serve the remaining marinade with the chicken.

note: When cooking with beer, it can be either dark or light, flat or not, chilled or at room temperature.

Even with a whole chicken, it's important to turn the bird on the grill several times to promote even cooking and browning. Resting time is extremely important for whole chickens cooked on the grill, as it gives the juices time to settle.

Roast Chicken with Lemon and Rosemary   *Serves 6 to 8*

2 SMALL ONIONS

4 SPRIGS FRESH ROSEMARY (2 ABOUT
   4 INCHES LONG AND WITH THICK,
   WOODY STEMS)

2 SMALL LEMONS

2 TABLESPOONS RICE WINE VINEGAR

1/4 CUP DIJON MUSTARD

2 TEASPOONS SALT

1 TEASPOON FRESHLY GROUND BLACK
   PEPPER

TWO 3- TO 3 1/2-POUND CHICKENS

VEGETABLE OIL COOKING SPRAY

1. Thinly slice 1 1/2 onions. Set the remaining 1/2 onion aside. Strip the leaves from the 2 smallest sprigs of rosemary; set the longer sprigs aside. Coarsely chop the rosemary leaves. Grate the zest from 1 lemon and juice the lemon.

2. Combine the sliced onion, chopped rosemary leaves, lemon zest, vinegar, mustard, the juice of the lemon with the zested rind, salt, and pepper in a small glass or ceramic bowl. Mix well.

3. Cut the remaining 1/2 onion into 2 wedges and 1/2 of the remaining lemon into 2 wedges. (Squeeze the leftover 1/2 lemon into the marinade.) Insert the woody sprigs of rosemary through the onion and lemon wedges, piercing them first with a small, sharp knife, if necessary.

4. Rub the marinade over the chickens and inside the cavities. Insert a rosemary "skewer" in each cavity. Put the chickens in a shallow pan, cover, and refrigerate for at least 2 hours or overnight.

5. Prepare a charcoal or gas grill, arranging the coals for indirect cooking. Lightly spray the grill rack with vegetable oil cooking spray. The coals should be moderately hot.

6. Place the chickens over the cooler part of the grill, cover and roast for 1 hour and 20 minutes to 1 hour and 30 minutes, turning with tongs at least 3 or 4 times during grilling. Cook until the juices run clear when the thigh is pierced with a fork or sharp knife, or an instant-read thermometer inserted in the thickest part of the thigh registers 180°F. Don't let the thermometer touch the bone. Add fresh coals to the fire as necessary to maintain a moderate, constant heat. If using a gas grill, adjust the burner furthest from the chicken to medium. Let the chicken sit for at least 10 minutes for the juices to collect. Remove the onion and lemon from the cavities before serving.

This roasted chicken is for garlic lovers only. The creamy garlic sauce that accompanies the chicken is strong—a little bit goes a long way, which is why the recipe yields only about half a cup. Making small "x" incisions in the garlic cloves before roasting promotes more thorough cooking so that their flavor is milder.

Ten-Clove Garlic-Roasted Chicken *Serves 4*

VEGETABLE OIL COOKING SPRAY

10 CLOVES GARLIC, PEELED

3 TABLESPOONS SNIPPED FRESH
   CHIVES

ONE 3- TO 3½-POUND CHICKEN

OLIVE OIL

FRESHLY GROUND BLACK PEPPER TO
   TASTE

¼ CUP HALF-AND-HALF

3 TABLESPOONS SOUR CREAM OR
   PLAIN YOGURT

2 TEASPOONS CHOPPED FLAT-LEAF
   PARSLEY OR CHIVES

SALT TO TASTE

1. Prepare a charcoal or gas grill, arranging the coals for indirect cooking. Lightly spray the grill rack with vegetable oil cooking spray. The coals should be moderately hot.

2. Using a small, sharp knife, cut an "x" incision halfway through each garlic clove, cutting from one end to the middle of the clove. Rub the outside of the chicken with 1 garlic clove. Insert all the garlic cloves and the chives in the cavity of the chicken. Rub the chicken with oil and pepper. Truss with kitchen twine.

3. Place the chicken over the cooler part of the grill, cover, and roast for 1 hour and 20 minutes to 1 hour and 30 minutes, turning with tongs 3 or 4 times. Cook until the juices run clear when the thigh is pierced with a fork or sharp knife, or an instant-read thermometer inserted in the thickest part of the thigh registers 180°F. Don't let the thermometer touch the bone. Add fresh coals to the fire as necessary to maintain a moderate heat. If using a gas grill, turn the burner away from the chicken to medium. Let the roast chicken sit for about 10 minutes for the juices to collect.

4. Remove the garlic from the chicken's cavity and transfer half of the cloves to a blender. Discard the remaining cloves. Add the half-and-half and sour cream and process until quite smooth. Scrape the sauce into a small bowl, stir in the parsley and season to taste with salt. Serve with the chicken.

Our recipes for boneless, skinless chicken breasts call for the amount to be determined by the number of breasts, rather than by weight. As a rule, six cutlets, or breast halves (3 whole breasts), weigh 2 to 2½ pounds. Although you can find breasts weighing less or more, they will generally fall into this range.

Lemon-Thyme Grilled Chicken Breasts *Serves 6*

JUICE OF 3 LEMONS

¼ CUP LOOSELY PACKED CHOPPED
FRESH THYME

1 LARGE CLOVE GARLIC, CRUSHED

FRESHLY GROUND BLACK PEPPER TO
TASTE

3 BONELESS, SKINLESS CHICKEN
BREASTS, TRIMMED AND HALVED

VEGETABLE OIL COOKING SPRAY

1. Combine the lemon juice, thyme, garlic, and a generous amount of pepper in a bowl, stirring well. Put the chicken breasts in a shallow glass or ceramic bowl and pour the marinade over them, turning to coat. Cover and refrigerate for at least 1 hour and as long as 6 hours.

2. Prepare a charcoal or gas grill. Lightly spray the grill rack with vegetable oil cooking spray. The coals should be moderately hot.

3. Lift the chicken from the marinade. Discard the marinade. Grill the chicken breasts for 12 to 16 minutes, turning with tongs several times, until cooked through. Serve immediately.

Many home cooks find buying boneless, skinless breasts easier than boning the chicken breasts themselves. Today, these are so popular they generally are fresh and tender, but beware of chicken that looks discolored or, under the plastic wrapping, is sitting in small puddles of water, which indicates freezing and thawing and refreezing. This treatment renders the chicken tough and rubbery.

Citrus-Marinated Grilled Chicken Breasts *Serves 6*

3 BONELESS, SKINLESS CHICKEN
   BREASTS, TRIMMED AND HALVED
SALT TO TASTE
1¼ CUPS FRESH ORANGE JUICE
3 TABLESPOONS FRESH LEMON JUICE
2 TEASPOONS GROUND GINGER
1¼ TEASPOONS DRIED THYME
2 TABLESPOONS SOY SAUCE
4 TABLESPOONS PLAIN DRIED BREAD
   CRUMBS
VEGETABLE OIL COOKING SPRAY

1. Sprinkle the chicken breasts lightly on both sides with salt and put the chicken in a glass or ceramic bowl.

2. Combine the orange juice, lemon juice, ginger, thyme, soy sauce, and bread crumbs in a glass or ceramic bowl, stirring to make a thin paste. Pour the paste over the chicken and rub it into the chicken. Cover and refrigerate for no longer than 6 hours.

3. Prepare a charcoal or gas grill. Lightly spray the grill rack with vegetable oil cooking spray. The coals should be moderately hot.

4. Put the chicken on the grill and cook for 12 to 16 minutes, turning with tongs several times, or until cooked through and the crumbs are browned. Serve immediately.

If you plan to grill a number of boneless, skinless chicken breasts, you will save money (if not time) by buying whole chicken breasts and boning and skinning them yourself. Remember that a chicken has only one breast and so what most people think of as a "chicken breast" is actually one half breast.

Grilled Chicken with Black Pepper and Goat Cheese *Serves 6*

3 BONELESS, SKINLESS CHICKEN
   BREASTS, TRIMMED AND HALVED
1/4 CUP OLIVE OIL
FRESHLY GROUND BLACK PEPPER TO
   TASTE
6 OUNCES SOFT GOAT CHEESE
3 TABLESPOONS SNIPPED CHIVES
SALT TO TASTE
VEGETABLE OIL COOKING SPRAY
1 SMALL HEAD BOSTON LETTUCE

1. Put the chicken breasts in a shallow glass or ceramic dish. Rub the chicken with olive oil and pepper. Cover and refrigerate for at least 30 minutes and for as long as 6 hours.

2. Combine the goat cheese and chives in a small bowl. Season with salt and pepper, blending well.

3. Prepare a charcoal or gas grill. Lightly spray the grill rack with vegetable oil cooking spray. The coals should be moderately hot to hot.

4. Grill the chicken for about 5 minutes. Turn the breasts over and spread about 1 tablespoon of the goat cheese mixture in a thin coat on each breast half. Cook for 7 to 11 minutes longer, without turning the chicken, or until the chicken is cooked through. About 1 minute before the chicken is done, use tongs to turn the breasts, so that the cheese side faces the fire and the cheese bonds to the meat. Serve immediately on a bed of lettuce, with the remaining goat cheese-chive mixture on the side.

Boneless, skinless chicken breast halves lend themselves nicely to stuffing and rolling—and cook beautifully on the grill. Flatten them with a gentle hand; you do not want to pound the tender meat into mush, but you do want an even thickness to facilitate rolling and cooking.

Grilled Chicken Breast Rolls with Olivada and Rosemary *Serves 4*

2 BONELESS, SKINLESS CHICKEN
  BREASTS, TRIMMED AND HALVED
1 TEASPOON FINELY CHOPPED FRESH
  ROSEMARY
¼ TEASPOON SALT
FRESHLY GROUND BLACK PEPPER TO
  TASTE
2 TABLESPOONS FRESH LEMON JUICE
2 TABLESPOONS OLIVE OIL
3 TABLESPOONS CHOPPED FLAT-LEAF
  PARSLEY
TOOTHPICKS OR SMALL METAL
  SKEWERS
VEGETABLE OIL COOKING SPRAY
4 TEASPOONS OLIVADA (SEE NOTE)

1. Cover the chicken breasts with waxed paper or plastic wrap and, using a meat mallet or small, heavy skillet, gently flatten the breasts to an even thickness of about $1/4$ inch.

2. Season the chicken breasts with the rosemary, salt, and pepper and put the breasts in a shallow glass or ceramic dish. Add the lemon juice and oil, turning to coat evenly. Cover and refrigerate for 2 to 4 hours. Meanwhile, soak wooden toothpicks in cold water for 30 minutes or plan to use small metal skewers to fasten the breasts closed.

3. Prepare a charcoal or gas grill. Lightly spray the grill rack with vegetable oil cooking spray. The coals should be moderately hot to hot.

4. Lift the breasts from the marinade. Discard the marinade. Place the breasts on a work surface and sprinkle evenly with parsley. Spread 1 teaspoon of olivada on each breast. Roll the breasts up jelly-roll style to make neat rolls. Fasten with wooden toothpicks.

5. Grill the rolls for 14 to 18 minutes, turning frequently with tongs, until the chicken is lightly browned, feels springy when touched, and the meat is cooked through. Serve immediately.

note: Olivada is a paste made mainly from Niçoise olives, olive oil, and seasonings and is sold in specialty stores.

Kabobs are favorites on the grill and for chicken kabobs, we recommend white breast meat, cut from boneless, skinless meat.

Honey-Mustard Chicken Kabobs   *Serves 6*

6 TABLESPOONS HONEY

1/4 CUP DIJON MUSTARD

3 TABLESPOONS LEMON JUICE

1 TABLESPOON CHOPPED FRESH THYME

SALT AND FRESHLY GROUND BLACK
    PEPPER TO TASTE

2- TO 2 1/4-POUNDS BONELESS, SKIN-
    LESS CHICKEN BREASTS, CUT INTO
    ABOUT THIRTY 1 1/2-INCH CHUNKS

VEGETABLE OIL COOKING SPRAY

1 LARGE GREEN BELL PEPPER, CUT
    INTO TWELVE 1 1/2-INCH CHUNKS

1 LARGE RED BELL PEPPER, CUT INTO
    TWELVE 1 1/2-INCH CHUNKS

3 LARGE PORTOBELLO MUSHROOMS,
    TRIMMED AND QUARTERED

SIX 12-INCH METAL SKEWERS

1. Combine the honey, mustard, lemon juice, and thyme in a shallow glass or ceramic bowl. Season with salt and pepper, stirring well. Add the chicken, tossing to coat. Cover and refrigerate for at least 3 hours and as long as 6 hours.

2. Prepare a charcoal or gas grill. Lightly spray the grill rack with vegetable oil cooking spray. The coals should be moderately hot to hot.

3. Lift the chicken from the marinade. Thread the chicken, peppers, and mushrooms on skewers, beginning and ending with peppers. Drizzle a little of the remaining marinade over the skewers. Grill, covered, for 10 to 12 minutes, turning often, until the chicken is cooked through, the peppers are charred, and the mushrooms are tender. Serve immediately.

When buying meat for kabobs, look for boneless chicken breasts, which may be called cutlets or even supremes; both terms refer to breasts. The term "supreme" was coined years ago by chefs (notably Escoffier) who considered these fillets quite fancy. Supremes usually include both the small and large fillets from the breast half—as do most packages labeled "cutlets" or "breasts."

Thai-Style Chicken Kabobs   *Serves 6*

2- TO 2¼-POUNDS BONELESS, SKIN-
    LESS CHICKEN BREASTS, CUT INTO
    ABOUT THIRTY 1½-INCH CHUNKS
3 LARGE RED OR GREEN BELL PEPPERS,
    CUT INTO 1½-INCH PIECES
3 TABLESPOONS CANOLA OIL
3 TABLESPOONS FRESH LIME JUICE
1½ TABLESPOONS SOY SAUCE
2 CLOVES GARLIC, FINELY CHOPPED
2 TABLESPOONS SHREDDED FRESH
    BASIL
2 TABLESPOONS SHREDDED CILANTRO
1 TABLESPOON LIGHT BROWN SUGAR
VEGETABLE OIL COOKING SPRAY
FOUR 12-INCH METAL SKEWERS

1. Combine the chicken and peppers in a glass or ceramic dish.

2. Combine the oil, lime juice, soy sauce, garlic, basil, cilantro, and brown sugar in a small bowl, mixing well. Add to the chicken and peppers, tossing to coat. Cover and refrigerate for 30 minutes or up to 6 hours.

3. Prepare a charcoal or gas grill. Lightly spray the grill rack with vegetable oil cooking spray. The coals should be moderately hot.

4. Thread the chicken and peppers onto skewers, beginning and ending with the peppers. Drizzle some marinade over the skewers. Grill, covered, for 10 to 12 minutes, turning with tongs several times, until the chicken is cooked through. Serve.

When skewered onto small bamboo skewers, chicken kabobs are great appetizers, welcome at any outdoor party. They can be served at room temperature.

Chicken Satay

Serves 3 as a main course; serves 6 as an appetizer

1½ POUNDS BONELESS, SKINLESS
   CHICKEN BREAST, TRIMMED

½ CUP RICE WINE VINEGAR

⅓ CUP CREAMY PEANUT BUTTER

2 TABLESPOONS SOY SAUCE

2 TABLESPOONS FRESH LIME JUICE

1 TABLESPOON PACKED LIGHT BROWN
   SUGAR

1 TABLESPOON CHOPPED FRESH GINGER

2 TO 3 SCALLIONS, WHITE AND GREEN
   PARTS, CHOPPED

4 TO 6 BAMBOO SKEWERS

VEGETABLE OIL COOKING SPRAY

1. Cut the chicken on the diagonal into 1-inch-wide strips.

2. Whisk together the vinegar, peanut butter, soy sauce, lime juice, sugar, ginger, and scallions in a glass or ceramic bowl. Add the chicken strips, tossing to coat. Cover and refrigerate for at least 1 hour or up to 6 hours.

3. Soak 4 to 6 bamboo skewers, depending on length and how you will serve the satay, in cold water to cover for 20 to 30 minutes.

4. Prepare a charcoal or gas grill. Lightly spray the grill rack with vegetable oil cooking spray. The coals should be moderately hot.

5. Thread the chicken onto the skewers, spearing each strip at least twice so that they are secure. Grill for 10 to 12 minutes, turning 2 or 3 times, until the chicken is cooked through. Serve immediately.

The grill makes chicken salads special by providing the meat with a slightly smoky flavor.

Cold Basil Pesto Chicken Salad

Serves 6

2½ CUPS TORN BASIL LEAVES

2 CLOVES GARLIC, COARSELY CHOPPED

3 TABLESPOONS GRATED PARMESAN CHEESE

2 TABLESPOONS CIDER VINEGAR

½ CUP EXTRA-VIRGIN OLIVE OIL

½ TEASPOON SALT

2- TO 2¼-POUNDS BONELESS SKINLESS CHICKEN BREAST HALVES, TRIMMED

VEGETABLE OIL COOKING SPRAY

RED LEAF LETTUCE

JUICE OF 1 LEMON

BASIL LEAVES, FOR GARNISH

1. Combine the basil, garlic, cheese, and vinegar in the bowl of a food processor. Pulse 3 or 4 times to mix. With the processor running, slowly add the olive oil through the feed tube until the pesto is well mixed. (It will be more liquid than pastelike.) Season with salt.

2. Put the chicken in a glass or ceramic bowl and pour the pesto marinade over it, turning several times to coat. Cover and refrigerate for at least 3 hours and as long as 6 hours.

3. Prepare a charcoal or gas grill. Lightly spray the grill rack with vegetable oil cooking spray. The coals should be moderately hot to hot.

4. Lift the chicken from the marinade, letting most of the marinade drip back into the bowl. Grill the chicken for 12 to 16 minutes, turning several times and brushing with the marinade once or twice during the first 5 minutes of cooking, until cooked through.

5. Let the chicken cool, cut into bite-sized pieces, and chill for at least 1 hour.

6. Arrange the lettuce on a serving platter and sprinkle with lemon juice. Spoon the chicken over the lettuce, garnish with basil leaves, and serve.

This chicken salad is a composed salad, which means each ingredient is tossed with the vinaigrette separately before being assembled on a serving platter. Like all chicken salads, this can be partially made ahead of time and then served at room temperature.

Mediterranean Grilled Chicken Salad *Serves 6*

SALAD

2 POUNDS BONELESS, SKINLESS
  CHICKEN BREAST HALVES, TRIMMED
WHITE WINE MARINADE (PAGE 189)
1 POUND SMALL RED POTATOES
1/2 POUND HARICOTS VERTS OR
  SLENDER GREEN BEANS, TRIMMED
VEGETABLE OIL COOKING SPRAY
12 TO 14 CHERRY TOMATOES, HALVED
  OR LEFT WHOLE, DEPENDING ON
  SIZE
2 TEASPOONS CHOPPED FRESH
  TARRAGON, FOR GARNISH

VINAIGRETTE

3/4 CUP EXTRA-VIRGIN OLIVE OIL
1/4 CUP WHITE WINE VINEGAR
2 TEASPOONS CHOPPED SHALLOTS
2 TEASPOONS DIJON MUSTARD
2 TEASPOONS CHOPPED FRESH
  TARRAGON
SALT AND FRESHLY GROUND BLACK
  PEPPER TO TASTE
FOUR TO SIX 12-INCH METAL SKEWERS

1. Place the chicken in a single layer in a shallow glass or ceramic dish and pour the marinade over it, turning a few times to coat. Cover and refrigerate for at least 1 hour and as long as 6 hours.

2. Put the potatoes in a saucepan and add cold water to cover by several inches. Bring to a boil over high heat and cook for 10 to 12 minutes just until fork tender. Drain and cool. Do not overcook.

3. Blanch the haricots verts in boiling water to cover for about 1 minute. Drain and cool.

4. Prepare a charcoal or gas grill. Lightly spray the grill rack with vegetable oil cooking spray. The coals should be moderately hot.

5. To make the vinaigrette, in a small bowl, whisk together the olive oil, vinegar, shallots, mustard, and tarragon. Season to taste with salt and pepper. Set aside.

6. Lift the chicken from the marinade. Discard the marinade. Grill the chicken for 12 to 16 minutes, turning several times, until cooked through. Slice into thin strips.

7. Thread the potatoes on metal skewers and grill for about 5 minutes until lightly browned. Cut into halves or quarters, depending on their size. Transfer to a bowl and toss with about 5 tablespoons of vinaigrette.

8. Meanwhile, in a separate bowl, toss the haricots verts with 3 or 4 tablespoons of vinaigrette. In another bowl, toss the cherry tomatoes with 3 or 4 tablespoons of vinaigrette.

9. Assemble the salad by spreading the beans on a platter. Top the beans with the potatoes and then the chicken. Arrange the tomatoes around the chicken and sprinkle the salad with tarragon. Drizzle a little vinaigrette over the salad and serve.

Chicken and citrus fruit blend very nicely in a salad that can be served warm or at room temperature.

Grilled Chicken-Citrus Salad with Arugula   *Serves 6*

½ CUP ORANGE JUICE

½ CUP GRAPEFRUIT JUICE

¼ CUP OLIVE OIL

3 TABLESPOONS MARMALADE

1 TABLESPOON FINELY CHOPPED FRESH
 GINGER

2 TABLESPOONS CHOPPED CILANTRO
 OR FLAT-LEAF PARSLEY

SALT AND FRESHLY GROUND BLACK
 PEPPER TO TASTE

2 TO 2¼ POUNDS BONELESS SKINLESS
 CHICKEN BREASTS, TRIMMED

VEGETABLE OIL COOKING SPRAY

1 ORANGE, PEELED

½ GRAPEFRUIT, PEELED

3 SCALLIONS, SLICED

1 LARGE HEAD RED OR GREEN LEAF
 LETTUCE

1 BUNCH ARUGULA

3 RED RADISHES, TRIMMED AND
 SLICED

CHOPPED CILANTRO, FOR GARNISH

1. Combine the juices, oil, marmalade, ginger, and cilantro in a shallow glass or ceramic dish. Season with salt and pepper, whisking well. Pour half the mixture into another bowl and set aside. Add the chicken to the dish, turning several times to coat. Cover and refrigerate for at least 1 hour and up to 6 hours.

2. Prepare a charcoal or gas grill. Lightly spray the grill rack with vegetable oil cooking spray. The coals should be moderately hot to hot.

3. Lift the chicken from the marinade and let most of it drip back into the dish. Grill the chicken for 12 to 16 minutes or until cooked through, turning several times; brush with any remaining marinade during the first 5 minutes of grilling. The chicken is done when the juices run clear when the thickest sections are pierced with a fork or sharp knife. Set aside to cool slightly.

4. Holding the fruit above a bowl, separate the orange and the grapefruit half into sections, letting any juices collect in the bowl. Drop the sectioned fruit into the bowl, add the scallions, and pour the reserved orange-marmalade dressing over the fruit. Toss gently. Cut the chicken into bite-sized pieces and add to the bowl. Toss to coat and season with salt and pepper.

5. Arrange the lettuce and arugula on a platter and top with the chicken mixture. Garnish with radishes and cilantro and serve.

Classic combinations such as sundried tomatoes and pine nuts are perfect foils for mild-flavored chicken, here tossed with pasta for a salad that can serve as main course or as part of an array of dishes at a picnic.

Grilled Chicken Pasta Salad with Sundried Tomatoes and Pine Nuts   *Serves 6*

SALAD

1½ POUNDS BONELESS, SKINLESS
   CHICKEN BREAST, TRIMMED

WHITE WINE MARINADE (PAGE 189)

10 TO 12 DRY-PACKED SUNDRIED
   TOMATOES

1 CUP BOILING WATER

VEGETABLE OIL COOKING SPRAY

¾ POUND FARFALLE, COOKED AL DENTE

6 TO 8 WATER-PACKED ARTICHOKE
   HEARTS (ONE 8½-OUNCE CAN),
   SLICED

6 TABLESPOONS TOASTED PINE NUTS
   (SEE NOTE)

1 ROASTED RED BELL PEPPER (PAGE
   203), SEEDED AND THINLY SLICED

1 ROASTED YELLOW BELL PEPPER
   (PAGE 203), SEEDED AND THINLY
   SLICED

2 TABLESPOONS CHOPPED FLAT-LEAF
   PARSLEY

1. Place the chicken in a single layer in a shallow glass or ceramic dish and pour the marinade over it. Turn a few times to coat, cover, and refrigerate for at least 1 hour and as long as 6 hours.

2. Cover the tomatoes with the water in a glass measuring cup and set aside to soak for 30 minutes. Drain, cool and slice into slivers. Set aside.

3. Prepare a charcoal or gas grill. Lightly spray the grill rack with vegetable oil cooking spray. The coals should be moderately hot.

4. To make the vinaigrette, whisk together the olive oil, vinegar, lemon juice, shallots, and parsley in a small bowl. Season to taste with salt and pepper. Set aside.

5. Lift the chicken from the marinade. Discard the marinade. Grill the chicken for 12 to 16 minutes, turning with tongs several times, until cooked through. Slice into thin strips.

VINAIGRETTE

¹/₄ CUP EXTRA-VIRGIN OLIVE OIL

2 TABLESPOONS WHITE WINE VINEGAR

1 TABLESPOON FRESH LEMON JUICE

¹/₂ TEASPOON CHOPPED SHALLOTS

2 TEASPOONS CHOPPED FLAT-LEAF
  PARSLEY

SALT AND FRESHLY GROUND BLACK
  PEPPER TO TASTE

6. Meanwhile, in a large serving bowl, toss the pasta with about ¹/₃ cup of the vinaigrette. Add the slivered tomatoes, artichoke hearts, pine nuts, and chicken. Toss to mix and add the peppers and parsley. Toss again, adjust the seasonings, and drizzle with more vinaigrette to taste. Serve at room temperature.

note: To toast the pine nuts, spread them in a dry skillet over medium-high heat for about 4 minutes until lightly browned and fragrant. Shake the pan during toasting to prevent burning. Transfer to a plate to cool completely. Alternatively, roast the pine nuts in a roasting pan in a 350°F oven until lightly browned and fragrant.

A chicken sandwich is even better when the chicken breast meat is grilled. Buy the best sourdough or Kaiser rolls you can find—preferably from a bakery—or use the soft rolls called potato rolls or Portuguese rolls. Good bread is crucial for a good sandwich.

Grilled Summer Chicken Sandwich with Roasted Red Peppers   *Serves 6*

3 BONELESS, SKINLESS CHICKEN
    BREASTS, TRIMMED AND HALVED
1 TABLESPOON CRACKED BLACK
    PEPPER
¼ CUP FRESH LEMON JUICE
2 TABLESPOONS COARSELY CHOPPED
    FRESH THYME OR TARRAGON
VEGETABLE OIL COOKING SPRAY
¼ CUP ROASTED GARLIC MAYONNAISE
    (PAGE 200) OR COMMERCIAL
    MAYONNAISE
6 SOURDOUGH OR KAISER ROLLS,
    HALVED
BIBB OR BOSTON LETTUCE
2 ROASTED RED BELL PEPPERS (SEE
    PAGE 203), CUT INTO STRIPS
SALT AND FRESHLY GROUND BLACK
    PEPPER TO TASTE

1. Cover chicken breasts with waxed paper or plastic wrap and, using a meat mallet or small, heavy skillet, gently flatten the breasts to an even thickness of about ½ inch. Put the meat in a shallow glass or ceramic dish.

2. Sprinkle both sides of the chicken with cracked pepper, pressing gently so that it adheres to the meat. Pour the lemon juice over the chicken and sprinkle with thyme. Cover and refrigerate for at least 1 hour and as long as 4 hours.

3. Prepare a charcoal or gas grill. Lightly spray the grill rack with vegetable oil cooking spray. The coals should be moderately hot to hot.

4. Grill the chicken for 10 to 14 minutes, turning several times, until cooked through.

5. Spread the mayonnaise on both halves of the rolls and place lettuce on the bottom halves of each roll. Top with strips of roasted red pepper. Place a chicken breast half on each sandwich, season with salt and pepper, and cover with the other half of the roll. Slice in half and serve immediately.

Rock Cornish game hens are tiny birds that have caught on with Americans, often connoting elegant dining. The miniature birds were the brainchild of poultry breeder Jacques Makowsky, who crossed Cornish game cocks with Plymouth Rock hens at his Connecticut farm. Since their debut in 1950, the tender hens have rapidly grown in popularity.

Grilled Moroccan-Style Rock Cornish Game Hens *Serves 4*

1/2 CUP PEANUT OIL

1/4 CUP FRESH LEMON JUICE

2 TABLESPOONS CHOPPED CILANTRO

2 TABLESPOONS CHOPPED FLAT-LEAF
  PARSLEY

2 CLOVES GARLIC, MINCED

1 TABLESPOON SWEET PAPRIKA

2 TEASPOONS GROUND CINNAMON

2 TEASPOONS GROUND TURMERIC

2 TEASPOONS GROUND ALLSPICE

2 TEASPOONS MINCED FRESH GINGER

2 TEASPOONS MINCED LEMON ZEST

FOUR 1- TO 1 1/4-POUND ROCK CORNISH
  GAME HENS

VEGETABLE OIL COOKING SPRAY

1. Combine the oil, lemon juice, cilantro, parsley, garlic, paprika, cinnamon, turmeric, allspice, ginger, and lemon zest in a small bowl and stir until well mixed.

2. Put the hens in a shallow glass or ceramic dish and pour the marinade over them. Rub it over the hens and inside the cavities. Using kitchen twine, truss the hens. Cover and refrigerate for at least 6 hours or overnight.

3. Prepare a charcoal or gas grill. Lightly spray the grill rack with vegetable oil cooking spray. The coals should be moderately hot.

4. Lift hens from the marinade. Discard the marinade. Grill, breast side down, for about 15 minutes. Turn and grill for 25 to 30 minutes longer, or until the juices run clear when the thickest part of the meat is pricked with a fork or sharp knife, and an instant-read thermometer inserted in the thickest meat registers 180°F. Let rest for about 5 minutes before serving.

Rock Cornish game hens are bred to be plump and all white meat—a combination that endears them to backyard chefs. Ask the butcher to flatten the hens for you or do it yourself. Treat these little treasures gently—they will flatten quite easily.

Coffee-Marinated Rock Cornish Game Hens   *Serves 4*

FOUR 1- TO 1¼-POUND ROCK CORNISH
   GAME HENS
4 CUPS STRONG BREWED COFFEE, AT
   ROOM TEMPERATURE
VEGETABLE OIL COOKING SPRAY
2 ANCHOVIES OR 2 TEASPOONS
   ANCHOVY PASTE
2 TABLESPOONS OLIVE OIL
SALT AND FRESHLY GROUND BLACK
   PEPPER TO TASTE
1 TO 2 TABLESPOONS CHOPPED FRESH
   ROSEMARY

1. Split the hens down the backbone and using your hands, flatten them. Put them in a large shallow glass or ceramic dish. Pour the coffee over them, cover, and refrigerate for 2 hours.

2. Prepare a charcoal or gas grill. Lightly spray the grill rack with vegetable oil cooking spray. The coals should be moderately hot.

3. Combine the anchovies and oil in a small bowl and mix, mashing the anchovies with a fork, to make a paste.

4. Lift the hens from the coffee marinade and pat dry with paper towels. Rub the hens all over with the anchovy-olive oil mixture, inserting a little under the skin. Season with salt and pepper and sprinkle the skin sides with rosemary. Reserve about ½ tablespoon rosemary for garnish.

5. Grill, breast side down, for about 15 minutes. Turn and grill for 25 to 30 minutes longer until the juices run clear when the thickest part of the meat is pricked with a fork or sharp knife, and an instant-read thermometer inserted in the thickest meat registers 180°F. The skin should be browned and crisp. Let rest for about 5 minutes before serving.

Once you roast a turkey out of doors—even in the dead of winter—you will become a convert. The meat has a slightly smoky flavor that is hard to resist. We recommend fresh turkey, and preferably one that has been raised naturally. We suggest relatively small turkeys for outdoor grilling—those weighing 16 pounds or more do best in the oven. But 12- or 14-pound birds are spectacular cooked outside, and having the turkey on the grill frees up the oven for other dishes, including the dressing that many feel is essential when serving turkey.

It's important to keep the fire relatively cool, which is why we suggest putting an oven thermometer in the grill if yours is not equipped with one. If using a charcoal grill, you will have to add fresh coals to the fire every forty-five minutes or so to maintain the heat. Keeping the vents only partially opened helps keep the fire low, too. We found that, as in the oven, the turkey requires very little tending. The drip pan filled with water provides a nice, moist environment that makes it unnecessary to baste the turkey. If you prefer, add chicken broth and wine to the water for a little more flavor. But truth be told, we find this makes very little difference as the overall taste of the bird is that of smokiness.

Roast Turkey On-the-Grill   *Serves 6 to 8*

VEGETABLE OIL COOKING SPRAY

ONE 12-POUND FRESH TURKEY

CANOLA OIL

SALT AND FRESHLY GROUND BLACK
   PEPPER TO TASTE

2 OR 3 CARROTS, COARSELY CHOPPED

1 LARGE ONION, COARSELY CHOPPED

2 CLOVES GARLIC, COARSELY CHOPPED

3 TABLESPOONS CHOPPED FLAT-LEAF
   PARSLEY

1 TABLESPOON CHOPPED FRESH THYME

1. Prepare a charcoal or gas grill, arranging the coals for indirect cooking. Lightly spray the grill rack with vegetable oil cooking spray. Set a drip pan filled halfway with water under the area of the rack where the turkey will sit. Position an oven thermometer inside the grill, cover, and let the temperature reach 350°F. The coals should be moderately hot, but will cool down when the turkey cooks.

2. Rub the turkey inside and out with oil. Season the turkey inside and out with salt and pepper. Stuff the cavity with the carrots, onion, garlic, parsley, and thyme.

3. Set the turkey on the rack over the drip pan. Cover and grill for 2^1/$_2$ to 3 hours, or for approximately 12 to 15 minutes to the pound. Maintain the internal temperature of the grill at 300° to

325°F. Add fresh coals to the fire after about 45 minutes as necessary to maintain a moderate, constant heat. If using a gas grill, adjust the burners to keep the temperature even. The turkey is done when a meat thermometer inserted in the thickest part of the thigh registers 180°F and the juices run clear when the meat is pierced with a fork or sharp knife.

4. Transfer the turkey to a platter or cutting board and let rest for 15 minutes before carving. Discard the vegetables in the turkey's cavity.

urkey producers have heeded the desires of consumers and stock the market with turkey parts, including ground turkey breast and boneless, skinless cutlets. Ask the butcher to cut the fillets into 4-ounce cutlets for you, if necessary. And as with chicken roulades, the cutlets should be pounded to an even thickness. This facilitates rolling and even cooking on the grill.

Turkey Roulades with Fontina, Prosciutto, and Pesto Butter   *Serves 8*

PESTO BUTTER

1/4 CUP UNSALTED BUTTER, SOFTENED

3 TABLESPOONS SUMMER PESTO (PAGE 181) OR COMMERCIAL PESTO

2 TABLESPOONS GRATED PARMESAN CHEESE

FRESHLY GROUND BLACK PEPPER TO TASTE

ROULADES

16 WOODEN TOOTHPICKS OR SMALL METAL SKEWERS

EIGHT 4-OUNCE BONELESS, SKINLESS TURKEY BREAST CUTLETS

SALT AND FRESHLY GROUND BLACK PEPPER TO TASTE

8 THIN SLICES PROSCIUTTO OR PARMA HAM

8 SLICES FONTINA CHEESE (ABOUT 4 OUNCES TOTAL)

OLIVE OIL

VEGETABLE OIL COOKING SPRAY

1. To prepare the pesto butter, combine the butter, pesto, and cheese in a small bowl. Mash with a fork until well mixed. Season to taste with pepper and scrape the butter onto a sheet of plastic wrap. Using your hands and the plastic wrap as guides, form the butter into a log. Wrap securely and refrigerate for at least 1 hour until firm. Meanwhile, soak the toothpicks in water for about 30 minutes or plan to use small metal skewers to fasten the breasts closed.

2. To prepare the roulades, cover the turkey cutlets with waxed paper or plastic wrap and, using a meat mallet or small, heavy skillet, gently flatten the cutlets into oval-shaped pieces about 1/4 inch thick. Transfer the cutlets to a wax paper-lined baking sheet. Season with salt and pepper. Place a slice of prosciutto on each cutlet, aligning the ham with the edges of the cutlet. Cut the pesto butter into 8 equal-sized pieces.

3. Place a piece of cheese and a slice of butter on the short end of each slice of prosciutto. Fold the prosciutto over the cheese and butter and then roll each cutlet into a neat package, tucking in the edges to enclose the stuffing. Secure each roulade with soaked wooden toothpicks. Leaving the roulades on the baking sheet, brush them with oil and refrigerate until ready to cook.

4. Prepare a charcoal or gas grill. Lightly spray the grill rack with vegetable oil cooking spray. The coals should be moderately hot.

5. Grill the roulades, turning frequently, for about 10 minutes, or until lightly browned. Cover the grill and cook for 3 or 4 minutes longer until the butter and cheese begin to ooze from the roulades and the meat is cooked through. Serve immediately.

$\mathbf{T}$he bland flavor of turkey makes it a natural for boldly flavored marinades and the accompaniments that typically are served with fajitas, Tex-Mex food at its best.

Grilled Turkey Fajitas *Serves 6*

¼ CUP FRESH LIME JUICE

2 TABLESPOONS PEANUT OIL

2 TABLESPOONS CHOPPED CILANTRO

1 TABLESPOON CHILI POWDER

1 TEASPOON GROUND CUMIN

½ TEASPOON CAYENNE PEPPER

SALT AND FRESHLY GROUND BLACK
    PEPPER

2 POUNDS BONELESS, SKINLESS
    TURKEY BREAST CUTLETS OR
    TENDERS

VEGETABLE OIL COOKING SPRAY

TWELVE 7-INCH FLOUR TORTILLAS

½ CUP CHOPPED, SEEDED TOMATOES

½ CUP CHOPPED AVOCADO

¼ CUP CHOPPED SCALLIONS

3 CUPS SHREDDED LETTUCE

CHOPPED CILANTRO, FOR GARNISH

SOUR CREAM, FOR GARNISH

BAJA-STYLE TOMATO SALSA (PAGE 185)
    OR HOT, HOT, HOT GRILLED SALSA
    (PAGE 186)

1. Combine the lime juice, oil, cilantro, chili powder, cumin, and cayenne in a glass or ceramic dish. Season with salt and pepper, stirring well. Put the turkey in the dish, turning several times to coat. Cover and refrigerate for 6 to 8 hours.

2. Prepare a charcoal or gas grill. Lightly spray the grill rack with vegetable oil cooking spray. The coals should be moderately hot.

3. Lift the turkey from the marinade. Discard the marinade. Grill the turkey for 10 to 14 minutes until cooked through, turning several times.

4. Meanwhile, wrap the tortillas in foil and place the packet on the outside edge of the grill and let the tortillas warm while the turkey cooks.

5. Cut the turkey into narrow strips and divide evenly among the warm tortillas. Top with tomatoes, avocado, scallions, lettuce, and cilantro and a dollop of sour cream and fold the tortillas around the filling. Serve with salsa.

urkey tenders are widely sold in supermarket meat departments and from butcher shops. They are the tender flap of meat that lies directly under the turkey breast. If you prefer, cut the tenders from the turkey breast yourself. They can weigh as much as 12 ounces and should be cut in half lengthwise to make six-ounce "steaks." For even cooking, pound the tenders gently to an even thickness.

Grilled Turkey Steaks *Serves 6*

2½ POUNDS TURKEY BREAST TEN-
    DERS, CUT LENGTHWISE IN HALF

1 CUP DRY SHERRY

¼ CUP FRESH LEMON JUICE

1 TABLESPOON GRATED ORANGE ZEST

2 TABLESPOONS HONEY

¼ TEASPOON GROUND CLOVES

2 TABLESPOONS DIJON MUSTARD

¼ TEASPOON CHILI POWDER

VEGETABLE OIL COOKING SPRAY

1. Place the tenders between sheets of waxed paper and, using a meat mallet or small, heavy skillet, gently flatten the breasts to an even thickness of about ½ inch.

2. Combine the sherry, lemon juice, orange zest, honey, cloves, mustard, and chili powder in a shallow glass or ceramic dish and mix well. Add the turkey steaks and turn to coat. Cover and refrigerate for at least 1 hour.

3. Prepare a charcoal or gas grill. Lightly spray the grill rack with vegetable oil cooking spray. The coals should be moderately hot.

4. Lift the turkey from the marinade and pat dry. Discard the marinade. Place the turkey on the grill, cover, and grill for about 16 minutes, turning several times, until cooked through, being careful not to overcook. Serve immediately.

CHAPTER 6

GAME AND GAME BIRDS

The grill is the most natural place to cook game and game birds. After all, since the discovery of fire, man has been cooking game over glowing embers and today, even with our sophisticated indoor cooking methods, the backyard grill is surprisingly similar to a primitive fire pit scraped from the packed dirt of a cave's entry. The ancient cooking method has not survived in vain, since, when properly handled, grilled game is delicious: delectably charred on the outside, juicy and tender on the inside, and with a vague smokiness augmenting its rich, gamy flavor.

By definition, the animals that fall in this category have better-developed muscle mass and eat a more varied and erratic diet than do animals raised domestically. This results in leaner meat that often is described as tasting "gamy." The gaminess pleases many folks and explains in part why thousands of Americans take to the woods, marshlands, and upland meadows in the fall and winter for hunting seasons. Much of the game eaten in the United States and Canada is the spoil of such sport, but a growing amount is raised on farms and preserves specifically for the retail market. Venison, rabbit, duck, pheasant, and quail are all available from farmers. In fact, butchers and other retailers cannot sell game meat that is not farm-raised. Any game shot by hunters cannot be marketed commercially—it is for personal consumption only.

Despite such regulations, farm-raised game and game birds retain much of their wild characteristics. To ensure this, farmers permit deer raised for venison to roam inside large fenced enclosures; ducks, pheasant, and quail, their wings clipped, are raised in open pens, as are rabbits. The natural environments provide most of the food, but these animals are also fed scientifically formulated feed designed to replicate the optimum diet they might find in the wild. They are slaughtered and butchered in safe, sanitary conditions and arrive at the retail market ready for consumers. Be sure to ask your butcher to prepare the game for the grill for you if you are not comfortable doing it yourself.

We find that most game benefits from oily marinades or at the very least a good rubbing with oil to keep it from drying out over the coals. We also like to pair the game with strong flavors that can stand up to its gusto. When cooking game and game birds, take care not to overcook the meat and to maintain the fire at the correct temperature, which for the recipes that follow is moderately hot—neither sizzling nor cool.

Preparing Game and Game Birds for Grilling

When you get the meat home from the butcher or supermarket, immediately stow it in the coldest part of the refrigerator, which usually is the rear of the lowest shelf. Do not unwrap it; you do not want it to be exposed to the air unnecessarily and keeping it wrapped in its original packaging is a good idea.

When you are ready to prepare the game for marinating, take it from the refrigerator and let it come to room temperature, which means leaving it on the counter for about thirty minutes. If it is a particularly hot, humid summer day, reduce the counter time. Pat the meat dry with paper towels and then either marinate it, rub it with dry rub, or otherwise prepare it for the grill. We have not instructed you to pat the meat dry before marinating, rubbing, or otherwise preparing it in every recipe because it is universally appropriate whenever game is grilled.

Although a great deal of the duck consumed in this country is hunted during duck season, the duck you buy from the butcher or the meat counter will be farm-raised and carefully regulated. The most commonly sold variety is white pekin, also known as Long Island duckling. Other kinds of duck commonly available are muscovy, domestic mallard, and mullard, which is a cross between muscovy and pekin. Whole white pekin ducks weigh from $4^1/_2$ to $5^1/_2$ pounds, have mild flavor and juicy meat, and are of a variety that originated centuries ago in China. Muscovy ducks are somewhat more flavorful than pekins and may be smaller, too. Mallards are far smaller than either (from $1^1/_2$ to 3 pounds) and are distinctively flavored with rich, dark meat. Mullards, larger than the white pekin, are bred to be meaty and juicy, with good duck flavor. Any variety of duck would work well in these recipes, which call only for the duck breast, considered the finest cut of the bird. In this recipe, we serve the duck skin cooked until crisp (cracklings). The skin is sinfully delicious and the same technique employed here can be used in the recipe for Grilled Duck Breast in Grapefruit and Chipotle Marinade with Grapefruit-Avocado Salad.

Grilled Mustard Duck Breast with Cracklings *Serves 4*

2 WHOLE BONELESS DUCK BREASTS,
   WITH SKIN
1 TABLESPOON OLIVE OIL
1 TABLESPOON BALSAMIC VINEGAR
1 CLOVE GARLIC, MINCED
2 TEASPOONS DIJON MUSTARD
1 TEASPOON BROWN SUGAR
1 TEASPOON DRIED THYME
1 TEASPOON FRESHLY GROUND PEPPER
$^1/_4$ TEASPOON SALT
VEGETABLE OIL COOKING SPRAY
4 FIRM TART APPLES, SUCH AS
   GRANNY SMITH, CORTLAND, OR
   WINESAP, QUARTERED AND CORED

1. Using your fingers and a small sharp knife, remove the skin from the duck breasts. Try to keep it in fairly large pieces. Refrigerate the skin until ready to cook.

2. Combine the oil, vinegar, garlic, mustard, brown sugar, and thyme in a shallow glass or ceramic dish. Season with pepper and salt. Stir well.

3. Trim the duck breasts of any remaining fat or tough connective tissue and pat dry with paper towels. Place the duck breasts in the marinade, turning several times to coat. Cover and refrigerate for 2 to 4 hours.

4. Preheat the oven to 375°F. Lightly spray a jelly roll pan or other shallow baking pan with vegetable oil cooking spray. Place the duck skin in the pan, outer side down, and spread it flat. Bake for about 20 minutes until browned and crisp. Drain on paper towels. Pour off all but 2 tablespoons of fat.

5. Raise the oven temperature to 400°F.

6. Place the apple quarters in a baking pan large enough to hold them snugly in one layer. Sprinkle the reserved 2 tablespoons of duck fat over the apples and toss to coat. Turn the quarters skin side down and bake for about 20 minutes, or until just tender.

7. Prepare a charcoal or gas grill. Lightly spray the grill rack with vegetable oil cooking spray. The coals should be moderately hot.

8. Lift the duck breasts from the marinade. Discard the marinade. Grill the breasts for about 5 minutes. Turn and grill for 3 or 4 minutes longer for medium-rare duck. For better-done meat, grill for a few minutes longer. Transfer the duck breasts to a cutting board and slice at an angle into wide, thin slices.

9. Meanwhile, cut the cracklings into thin slices or dice. Serve the duck meat with cracklings sprinkled over them and the apples alongside.

note: If the cracklings soften when it is time to serve them, crisp them in a 200°F oven for about 10 minutes right before serving.

ore than half of the ducks sold in this country are sold frozen, which is unfortunate because fresh duck tastes far better than frozen. Ask your butcher if he can get fresh duck for you—you won't be disappointed. If you buy frozen duck, let it defrost in the refrigerator for a day or two. When it is thawed, let it come to room temperature before wiping it dry with a paper towel and proceeding with the recipe.

Domestic ducks are marketed at ages between two and four months and so the consumer rarely has to worry about buying an old duck, which is tough and dry. If there is a question and if you have the opportunity to see the whole duck, look for soft pliable beaks, smooth legs, and soft webbing between the toes.

Grilled Duck Breast in Grapefruit and Chipotle Marinade with Grapefruit-Avocado Salad   *Serves 4*

DUCK

1 CHIPOTLE CHILI IN ADOBO SAUCE, WIPED DRY

ABOUT 1/2 TO 1 CUP CIDER VINEGAR

2 WHOLE BONELESS, SKINLESS DUCK BREASTS (SEE NOTE)

1/2 CUP FRESH GRAPEFRUIT JUICE

2 TABLESPOONS OLIVE OIL

2 CLOVES GARLIC, MINCED

1 TEASPOON DRIED OREGANO

1/4 TEASPOON SALT

VEGETABLE OIL COOKING SPRAY

1. To prepare the duck, soak the chili, which has been wiped dry, for about 10 minutes in hot water to cover. Drain and transfer to a small glass or ceramic dish, cover with vinegar, and set aside to marinate for at least 20 minutes. Drain and chop coarsely. You will have about 2 tablespoons of chopped chili.

2. Trim the duck breasts of any remaining fat or tough connective tissue and pat dry with paper towels. Score the skin side of the breasts in a diamond pattern.

3. Put the breasts in a shallow glass or ceramic dish. Combine the juice, oil, garlic, oregano, salt, and chopped chili in a bowl, stirring well. Add the marinade to the meat, turning to coat. Cover and refrigerate for 2 to 4 hours.

GRAPEFRUIT-AVOCADO SALAD

1 LARGE RED GRAPEFRUIT

½ BULB FENNEL, THINLY SLICED

1 LARGE AVOCADO, HALVED, PEELED,
    AND SLICED

1 TABLESPOON OLIVE OIL

SALT TO TASTE

4. Prepare a charcoal or gas grill. Lightly spray the grill rack with vegetable oil cooking spray. The coals should be moderately hot.

5. To make the salad, peel the grapefruit, trimming the white pith. Holding the fruit over a glass or ceramic bowl, slice the segments from the membrane, and let the juices drip into the bowl. Set the segments aside. Squeeze any juice from the membranes or peel into the bowl.

6. Toss the fennel with 1 or 2 tablespoons of the grapefruit juice and the olive oil in a small bowl. Season with salt.

7. Sprinkle the remaining juice over the avocado slices to prevent discoloration. Cut the avocado slices crosswise into thin slices. Arrange the fennel on a serving plate and top with the avocado and grapefruit slices.

8. Lift the duck breasts from the marinade. Discard the marinade. Grill the breasts for about 5 minutes. Turn and grill for 3 or 4 minutes longer for medium-rare meat. For better-done meat, grill for a few minutes longer. Transfer the duck breasts to a cutting board and slice at an angle into wide, thin slices. Serve the duck slices alongside the salad.

note: Chipotle chilies usually are sold canned, packed in adobo sauce, and are available in many supermarkets as well as Latin markets and specialty food stores. They are also available loose and dried, but are not as easy to find this way.

If you desire, reserve the duck skin and make cracklings, as explained in the recipe for Grilled Mustard Duck Breast with Cracklings on page 157. Serve them sprinkled over the duck slices.

Pheasant is similar to chicken in size and conformation, although it is drier and stronger tasting. The meat on most birds is finely textured, firm, and plentiful.

Pheasant with Juniper, Sage, Caraway, and Cider Marinade

Serves 4

ONE 2¹/₂- TO 3-POUND PHEASANT

¹/₂ CUP CHOPPED ONIONS

¹/₂ CUP COARSELY CHOPPED PARSLEY STEMS

1¹/₂ TEASPOONS FINELY CHOPPED FRESH SAGE

6 WHOLE JUNIPER BERRIES, CRUSHED

¹/₂ TEASPOON CRUSHED DRIED FENNEL SEED

1 CLOVE GARLIC, CRUSHED

¹/₄ TEASPOON BLACK PEPPERCORNS

¹/₂ CUP APPLE CIDER

¹/₄ CUP OLIVE OIL

1 TABLESPOON APPLE CIDER VINEGAR

VEGETABLE OIL COOKING SPRAY

1. Split the pheasant down the back along the backbone, taking care to keep the thigh meat intact. Remove the backbone. Cut through the top of the breast bone so that the breast can be flattened. Put the pheasant in a glass or ceramic dish, spreading it open and flattening the breast slightly. Rub the pheasant inside and out with onions, parsley, sage, juniper berries, fennel, garlic, and peppercorns. Add the cider, oil, and vinegar and turn the pheasant to coat evenly. Cover and refrigerate for at least 6 hours or overnight.

2. Prepare a charcoal or gas grill. Lightly spray the grill rack with vegetable oil cooking spray. The coals should be moderately hot.

3. Lift the pheasant from the marinade. Discard the marinade. Put the pheasant skin side down on the grill, cover, and cook for about 10 minutes. Turn the pheasant, cover the grill, and cook for about 10 minutes longer until the breast meat is cooked through, feels springy to the touch, and the juices run clear when pierced with a small sharp knife. Remove the pheasant from the grill and cut the thighs and legs from the pheasant. Return the thighs and legs to the grill and cook, turning several times, for 4 or 5 minutes longer until cooked through. (Let the breast meat rest while cooking the dark meat.) Serve immediately.

Pheasant are favorites of upland game hunters, but those at the butchers are farm-raised. Hens weigh less than cocks, which can weigh up to five pounds.

Pheasant with Orange Sauce

Serves 4

PHEASANT

ONE 2½- TO 3-POUND PHEASANT

1 TABLESPOON FINELY CHOPPED FRESH
    GINGER

1 TEASPOON CRUSHED CORIANDER
    SEED

1 TEASPOON COARSELY GROUND BLACK
    PEPPER

¼ CUP ORANGE JUICE

2 TABLESPOONS LIGHT SOY SAUCE

1 TEASPOON MOLASSES

VEGETABLE OIL COOKING SPRAY

SAUCE

2 CUPS ORANGE JUICE

1 CUP CHAMPAGNE VINEGAR

½ CUP GRANULATED SUGAR

¼ CUP FRESH LEMON JUICE

1 TABLESPOON FINELY CHOPPED FRESH
    GINGER

½ CUP REDUCED-SODIUM CHICKEN
    STOCK

2 TABLESPOONS FINELY SLIVERED
    GRATED ORANGE ZEST

1. Split the pheasant down the back along the backbone, taking care to keep the thigh meat intact. Remove the backbone. Cut through the top of the breast bone so that the breast can be flattened. Put the pheasant in a glass or ceramic dish, spreading it open and flattening the breast slightly. Rub the pheasant inside and out with ginger, coriander, and pepper. Add the orange juice, soy sauce, and molasses and turn the pheasant to coat evenly. Cover and refrigerate for at least 6 hours or overnight.

2. For the sauce, combine the orange juice, vinegar, sugar, lemon juice, and ginger. Bring to a boil over medium-high heat, stirring. Reduce the heat and simmer for about 10 minutes or until the sauce is reduced by half. Strain the sauce through a fine sieve and then return it to the pan. Add the chicken stock and orange zest and simmer for about 10 minutes longer, stirring, until the sauce is slightly syrupy. Serve warm or at room temperature with the pheasant.

3. Prepare a charcoal or gas grill. Lightly spray the grill rack with vegetable oil cooking spray. The coals should be moderately hot.

4. Lift the pheasant from the dish and discard the marinade. Put the pheasant on the grill skin side down, cover, and cook for 10 minutes. Turn the pheasant, cover and cook for 10 minutes longer until the breast meat is cooked through and the juices run clear when pierced with a small sharp knife. Remove the pheasant from the grill and cut off the thighs and legs. Return them to the grill while the breast meat rests and cook, turning several times, for 4 or 5 minutes longer until cooked through. Serve.

hese tiny birds can weigh from three-and-a-half to eight ounces, although for the best flavor, we suggest smaller birds. Their white meat is delicately flavored and quite skimpy; the dark meat is not worth thinking about since there is so little on the birds. Serve at least two quail per person, although if you are grilling for big eaters, consider three or more.

Grilled Quail with Raspberry-Cranberry Cumberland Sauce *Serves 4*

QUAIL

EIGHT 3½- TO 4-OUNCE QUAILS

4 TABLESPOONS FINELY CHOPPED
 SHALLOTS

2 TEASPOONS FINELY CHOPPED FRESH
 ROSEMARY

FRESHLY GROUND BLACK PEPPER TO
 TASTE

½ CUP OLIVE OIL

¼ CUP RASPBERRY VINEGAR

8 SMALL BAMBOO SKEWERS

VEGETABLE OIL COOKING SPRAY

SAUCE

¼ CUP SEEDLESS RASPBERRY JAM

¼ CUP PORT WINE

1 TABLESPOON CHOPPED SHALLOTS

½ TEASPOON GRATED LEMON ZEST

½ CUP FRESH ORANGE JUICE

½ CUP FRESH CRANBERRIES

1 TABLESPOON SUGAR

PINCH CAYENNE PEPPER

1. Using a small sharp knife or poultry shears, split each quail along the backbone, cutting through the ribs as close to the back-bone as possible. Open the quails, skin side down, and cut partway through the breastbone. Flatten the quails with the flat side of a cleaver or the heel of your hand. Put the quails in a large glass or ceramic dish. Rub each bird inside and out with the shallots, rosemary, and pepper. Pour the oil and vinegar over the birds, turning them to coat evenly. Cover and refrigerate for 4 hours or overnight.

2. To prepare the sauce, in a small saucepan combine the jam, port, shallots, and lemon zest. Bring to a simmer over medium-high heat. Reduce the heat and simmer gently for about 2 minutes. Add the orange juice, cranberries, and sugar, raise the heat to medium-high, and cook, stirring, for about 5 minutes, or until the cranberries burst and the sauce is slightly thickened. Season to taste with cayenne. Serve warm or at room temperature. (The sauce can be reheated just before serving.) Soak the bamboo skewers in warm water for at least 30 minutes.

3. Prepare a charcoal or gas grill. Lightly spray the grill rack with vegetable oil cooking spray. The coals should be moderately hot.

4. Lift the quail, one at a time, from the dish, and place each bird flat, positioning the legs and thighs pointing inward to frame the breast. Discard the marinade. Using bamboo skewers, skewer the quails so that they will hold together during grilling. Catch the outer skin of 1 thigh with a bamboo skewer and then weave it under the thigh bone, through the ribs and into the opposite thigh, over the bone and out through the center of the skin. Cut the skewer so that it juts from the bird no more than 1 inch. Repeat with the remaining quails.

5. Place the quails on the grill, skin sides down, and cover the grill. Cook for about 5 minutes, taking care the fire does not flare up or get too hot. Turn the birds and grill, covered, for about 5 minutes longer or until the breast meat feels springy to the touch and the meat is cooked through. Serve with the sauce.

To grill minute birds such as quail, it is a good idea to split them and spread them open so that they can lie nearly flat on the grill rack. They benefit from marinating—and will dry out quickly if overcooked.

Grilled Herb-Marinated Quail

Serves 4

EIGHT 3½- TO 4-OUNCE QUAILS

4 TO 6 CLOVES GARLIC, CRUSHED

2 TEASPOONS CHOPPED FRESH THYME LEAVES

1 TEASPOON DRIED OREGANO

1 TEASPOON SALT

16 JUNIPER BERRIES, CRUSHED

½ CUP DRY WHITE WINE

½ CUP OLIVE OIL

8 SMALL BAMBOO SKEWERS

VEGETABLE OIL COOKING SPRAY

1. Using a small sharp knife or poultry shears, split each quail along the backbone, cutting through the ribs as close to the backbone as possible. Open the quails, skin-side down, and cut through the breastbone. Flatten the quails using the flat side of a cleaver or the heel of your hand. Put the quails in a large glass or ceramic dish. Rub each bird inside and out with the garlic and then the thyme, oregano, salt, and juniper berries. Add the wine and oil to the birds, turning them to coat evenly. Cover and refrigerate for 4 hours or overnight.

2. Prepare a charcoal or gas grill. Lightly spray the grill rack with vegetable oil cooking spray. The coals should be moderately hot. Soak the bamboo skewers in warm water for at least 30 minutes.

3. Lift each quail, one at a time, from the dish, and place each bird flat, positioning the legs and thighs pointing inward to frame the breast. Discard the marinade. Using bamboo skewers, skewer the quails so that they will hold together during grilling. Catch the outer skin of 1 thigh with a bamboo skewer and then weave it under the thigh bone, through the ribs and into the opposite thigh, over the bone and out through the center of the skin. Cut the skewer so that it juts from the bird no more than 1 inch.

4. Place the quails on the grill, skin sides down, and cover the grill. Cook for about 5 minutes, taking care the fire does not flare up or get too hot. Turn the birds and grill, covered, for about 5 minutes longer or until the meat is cooked through. Serve immediately.

The venison loin is preferred for most culinary purposes, and certainly for grilling, although the haunch and saddle are good for moist indoor cooking, such as braising and stewing. Venison is leaner than other meat and so needs to be rubbed with oil before it is grilled. It also stands up very well to marinating. Try it with either of the wine-based marinades on pages 188 and 189. Venison loin steaks are all approximately the same size and weight.

Grilled Venison Loin Steaks with Red Wine-Herb Sauce   *Serves 6*

6 BONELESS VENISON LOIN STEAKS,
    EACH ABOUT $1/2$ INCH THICK
1 TEASPOON FINELY CHOPPED FRESH
    ROSEMARY
1 TEASPOON COARSELY GROUND BLACK
    PEPPER
2 TABLESPOONS OLIVE OIL
VEGETABLE OIL COOKING SPRAY
RED WINE–HERB SAUCE (PAGE 178)

1. Rub the venison steaks on both sides with the rosemary and pepper and put in a shallow glass or ceramic dish. Drizzle the olive oil over the meat, turning the steaks to coat. Cover and refrigerate for at least 2 hours or overnight.

2. Prepare a charcoal or gas grill. Lightly spray the grill rack with vegetable oil cooking spray. The coals should be moderately hot.

3. Grill the venison steaks for about 3 minutes on each side for rare meat. Grill for a few minutes longer for medium-rare or medium-done meat. Serve immediately with the wine sauce.

Rabbits are widely eaten in Europe, but have been slow to catch on here—except among rabbit hunters. This is a shame as rabbit meat is tender with a lovely gamy flavor. All rabbit sold by butchers or in the markets are farm-raised. Some rabbits weigh as little as two pounds, although we sell larger ones that might weigh as much as four pounds. If necessary, buy two smaller rabbits to achieve the right weight for the recipe.

Rabbit with Herb and Mustard Marinade

Serves 4 to 6

ONE 3½- TO 4-POUND RABBIT

¼ CUP DIJON MUSTARD

¼ CUP OLIVE OIL

1 TABLESPOON CHOPPED FRESH THYME

1 TABLESPOON FINELY CHOPPED GARLIC

2 TEASPOONS GRATED ORANGE ZEST

2 TEASPOONS GRATED LEMON ZEST

1 TEASPOON FRESHLY GROUND BLACK PEPPER

VEGETABLE OIL COOKING SPRAY

1. Rinse the rabbit in cold water and drain. Pat dry with paper towels. Sever the forelegs and hind legs from the body at the joints. Cut the center section, called the saddle, into 4 equal-sized pieces. Put the pieces in a shallow glass or ceramic dish large enough to hold them in a single layer.

2. Combine the mustard, oil, thyme, garlic, orange and lemon zest, and pepper in a small bowl, stirring well. Pour the marinade over the rabbit, turning to coat. Cover and refrigerate for 4 hours or overnight.

3. Prepare a charcoal or gas grill. Lightly spray the grill rack with vegetable oil cooking spray. The coals should be moderately hot.

4. Lift the meat from the marinade. Discard the marinade. Grill the rabbit for about 10 minutes, turning often until browned on all sides. Cover the grill and continue to cook for about 8 minutes. Turn the meat and grill for 5 to 7 minutes longer, or until cooked through. Move the smaller pieces of rabbit to the edge of the grill, if necessary, to prevent burning during cooking. If using a gas grill, reduce the heat a little to prevent burning. Serve immediately.

Rabbit is now quite easily available in supermarkets, although you may have to order it from the resident butcher. For grilling, we recommend cutting the rabbit into eight pieces. Uncooked rabbit meat is white, but when marinated and cooked, it turns dark.

Spicy-Marinated Grilled Rabbit   *Serves 4 to 6*

ONE 3¹/₂- TO 4-POUND RABBIT

1 CUP OLIVE OIL

2 TABLESPOONS CHOPPED FLAT-LEAF PARSLEY

1 TABLESPOON HOT PEPPER SAUCE

2 TEASPOONS MINCED GARLIC

1 TEASPOON DRIED ROSEMARY

¹/₂ TEASPOON SALT

¹/₂ TEASPOON FRESHLY GROUND BLACK PEPPER

VEGETABLE OIL COOKING SPRAY

1. Rinse the rabbit in cold water and drain. Pat dry with paper towels. Sever the forelegs and hind legs from the body at the joints. Cut the center section, called the saddle, into 4 equal-sized pieces. Put the pieces in a shallow glass or ceramic dish large enough to hold them in a single layer.

2. Combine the oil, parsley, hot pepper sauce, garlic, rosemary, salt, and pepper in a bowl, stirring well. then pour the marinade over the rabbit. Turn to coat, cover, and refrigerate for 4 hours or overnight.

3. Prepare a charcoal or gas grill. Lightly spray the grill rack with vegetable oil cooking spray. The coals should be moderately hot.

4. Lift the meat from the marinade. Discard the marinade. Grill the rabbit for about 10 minutes, turning often until browned on all sides. Cover the grill and continue to cook for about 8 minutes. Turn the meat and grill for 5 to 7 minutes longer, or until cooked through. Move the smaller pieces of rabbit to the edge of the grill, if necessary, to prevent burning during cooking. If using a gas grill, reduce the heat a little to prevent burning. Serve immediately.

note: Ask the butcher to cut up the rabbit for you, if you prefer.

CHAPTER 7

SAUCES, SALSAS, MARINADES, RUBS, AND OTHER CONDIMENTS

othing livens up a backyard meal like a full-flavored sauce, salsa, or other condiment. The right barbecue sauce, spicy salsa, or seasoned mayonnaise can make the difference between a bland meal and an exciting one. The same claims can be made for marinades, rubs, and pastes, which flavor the meat before grilling, providing herbal, citrusy, spicy, or sweet accents that happily mingle on our tongues when the meat is lifted from the grill.

Throughout the book, we incorporate marinades, rubs, and sauces in specific recipes, but just as often, we refer the reader to a recipe in this chapter. The distinction is made by the universality of the marinade or rub, defined by how adaptable it is. This does not mean you cannot use a marinade or rub you discover as part of a recipe with another kind of meat, but the formulas that follow here are particularly accommodating.

Meat and poultry can stand up to long marinating, although boneless chicken breasts and pork tenderloins should not be left soaking for more than four to six hours or their consistencies will be mushy. If you are in a hurry, pour the marinade over the meat and leave the meat at room temperature for a short time. Safety dictates that you never leave any kind of meat at room temperature for longer than one hour, which is why we generally instruct you to refrigerate the meat during soaking. Never reuse a marinade and never serve it as sauce with the grilled food without first boiling it for at least five full minutes to kill any bacteria. If you want, brush a little on the meat during the initial stages of grilling so that it can cook.

Marinades work because of the acid in them, supplied most commonly by vinegar, wine, cider, citrus juices, and tomatoes. Most contain a little oil, too, which lubricates the meat and acts as a flavor conductor. In ancient days, marinades were salty and were relied upon to preserve meat—but in the late twentieth century, this is hardly necessary (although this ancient application does explain the origin of the word, with its root in the Latin word for the sea). We do not marinate all meat. In fact, high-quality, tender cuts such as sirloin, hanger steak, rack of lamb, and veal chops are best when only minimally seasoned before grilling.

Marinades penetrate about one-quarter of an inch into the food—they don't infuse the meat to its center—and because of this, long marinating rarely accomplishes better flavor than the minimum time suggested. Longer marinating times are for convenience only. For example, we feel better organized when the meat and its marinade are successfully blended and tucked away in the 'fridge, leaving the remainder of the day free to tend to the rest of the meal.

Dry rubs and pastes are sometimes called "dry marinades," and as far as we are concerned, are still the best-kept secrets to great grilling. As a rule, they are packed with flavor derived from chilies and whole toasted spices. The seasoning mixtures are rubbed into the meat; the meat is then refrigerated in a dish or sealable plastic bag and allowed to "marinate in its own juices." This happens because the spice, sugar, or salt in the dry rub attracts moisture from deep within the meat to its surface, where it mixes with the rub or paste, forming a wet, sticky coating with a wallop of flavor. For the best flavor, pork, particularly ribs, and bone-in chicken can be rubbed up to twenty-four hours before grilling, while chops and steaks should not be left for longer than forty-five minutes at room temperature before they are grilled. During grilling, the dry rub forms an appealing crust on the meat, which is deliciously apparent in grilled meats such as spareribs.

Before pouring a marinade over meat or poultry, or before rubbing the spice mixture into the meat, pat the meat dry with paper towels. Put the food in a nonreactive dish (glass or ceramic is our choice), cover it with a lid or plastic wrap, and stow it in the refrigerator. As we have said, we also like to use heavy-duty plastic bags with zip closures, which are easier to store in a crowded refrigerator and easy to transport.

Hot Pepper Sauces

Supermarket shelves bulge with bottled hot sauces. No longer are Tabasco and Frank's Original Red Hot the only choices. When they were, life was easier but not always inspiring. Now, the choices may be mind-boggling, but the mouth-watering variety makes cooking even more fun.

The category of Asian hot sauces is perhaps the most exciting. Bottles and jars of chili paste, chili-garlic sauce, and similar flavoring agents, most often imported from Thailand and Vietnam, are common condiments on tables throughout Southeast Asia and are showing up here in large numbers, too. They are prepared mixtures of vinegar, salt, and chilies, and sometimes include garlic or sugar, or both, and vary significantly in degrees of heat. Experiment with these delightful condiments. They'll add seductive interest to your cooking, particularly when making barbecue sauces and marinades.

Why Marinate?

Although some veteran grill cooks prefer to cook meat virtually unadorned and then liven it up later with sauces and salsas, we like to use marinades because they add both flavor and fun to the process. Marinades can be made from tantalizing combinations of herbs, spices, and other flavorings, and can get your mouth watering just thinking about them. As far as we're concerned, half the fun of planning a grilling meal is conjuring up the marinade.

All marinades include an acid. Most commonly, this is wine, vinegar, tomatoes, or citrus juices. Theoretically, the acid breaks down fibers in the meat and tenderizes it, although the quality of meat available today often makes this unnecessary. However, the acid also infuses the food with tangy flavor. Most marinades are accented, too, with wonderfully bright flavors provided by spices, onions, garlic, chilies, mustards, peppers, and similar ingredients. The small amount of oil usually found in marinades serves a dual purpose—it adds moisture and serves as a flavor conductor.

The acid present in all marinades reacts with aluminum, which can impart a metallic taste to the food. Because of this, it is advisable to marinate all food in nonreactive containers. We prefer glass or ceramic, although some people marinate food in sturdy plastic containers with fitted lids, which works very well. Heavy plastic bags with secure zipped closures work well, too, and make it easy to "fit" the marinating meat in a crowded refrigerator.

Most meats can stand up to long marinating, although long baths do not intensify flavor. Marinades penetrate a mere one-quarter of an inch into the meat and after two, four, or six hours the food has absorbed as much of the marinade as it will. However, leaving the food to soak for as long as 24 hours frees your time and helps with organization. Tender cuts such as boneless chicken breasts and pork tenderloins should not be marinated for longer than specified in the recipe.

For safety, marinate food in the refrigerator. Turn it several times to coat it well and then cover the dish with plastic or a lid. During marinating, turn the meat several times, unless you feel confident it is totally submerged in liquid. Before grilling, let the meat or poultry reach room temperature—usually accomplished by letting it sit at room temperature for about 30 minutes.

We also strongly urge you to exercise caution when basting grilling meat or poultry with the marinade. We suggest doing so only during the first minutes of cooking. You want to leave ample time for the heat of the fire to destroy any harmful bacteria lurking in the marinade, usually imparted by the meat during soaking. If you want to use the marinade as a sauce once the meat is cooked, be sure to bring the marinade to a rapid boil and then simmer briskly for at least five minutes first. When in doubt, discard the marinade after it has done its initial job of flavoring the uncooked meat or poultry.

Fresh or Dry Herbs?

We like to use fresh herbs when we cook, although there are times when dried are preferable or at least acceptable. Fresh herbs grow in profusion in the warm months of the year and are easy to find in the markets. You may even have lush basil, thyme, tarragon, and rosemary plants flourishing in your garden or in pots on the patio, ready for snipping when a recipe beckons. Additionally, fresh herbs are full of moisture and therefore do not burn during grilling as easily as dried.

Dried herbs are more intensely flavored. The rule of thumb is to use about a third as much of a dried herb as fresh: a teaspoon of dried for every tablespoon of chopped fresh. When adding dried herbs to a marinade, sauce, or any other preparation, rub it between your fingers or in the palm of your hand to release its essential oils. Finally, store dried herbs in cool, dark cupboards and replenish them every six months, as they tend to go stale and lose flavor.

Although we call for specific herbs in our recipes, feel free to experiment with substitutions. Don't let the lack of cilantro, for example, dissuade you from making a salsa. Substitute parsley instead. Use thyme or chervil in place of tarragon; the flavor will be slightly different but the herb will still add great taste.

We sell a bottled barbecue sauce very similar to this one in our New York shop, which is on Madison Avenue near the corner of Eighty-second Street. It's great on beef, pork, or chicken. If you prefer hotter sauce, increase the amount of cayenne. Barbecue sauce is meant to be served with the cooked meat, not used as a marinade. However, you can slather it on chicken breasts or pork chops a few minutes before they are ready to come off the grill. If you do, then you can call it a "moppin" sauce.

Madison Avenue Barbecue Sauce

Makes about 1³/₄ cups

1 CUP TOMATO SAUCE

³/₄ CUP HONEY

³/₄ CUP SOY SAUCE

6 TABLESPOONS DISTILLED WHITE
   VINEGAR

¹/₄ CUP LIGHT CORN SYRUP

3 TABLESPOONS WORCESTERSHIRE
   SAUCE

2 TABLESPOONS HOISIN SAUCE

¹/₂ TEASPOON CAYENNE PEPPER

SALT AND FRESHLY GROUND BLACK
   PEPPER TO TASTE

Combine the ingredients in a nonreactive saucepan, stir, and cook over medium heat for about 30 minutes, or until the flavors blend. Let cool and use immediately, or cover and refrigerate for up to 5 days.

Most barbecue sauce recipes for the home cook have a catsup base, such as this one. Bottled catsup is a boon for backyard chefs, because it can easily be doctored up in so many ways.

Quick Barbecue Sauce   *Makes about ²/₃ cup*

2 TABLESPOONS CANOLA OIL

2 CLOVES GARLIC, FINELY CHOPPED

½ CUP CATSUP

2 TABLESPOONS CIDER VINEGAR

1 TEASPOON HOT PEPPER SAUCE

2 TEASPOONS PACKED LIGHT OR DARK
    BROWN SUGAR

2 TEASPOONS DIJON MUSTARD

Heat the oil in a small nonreactive saucepan over medium heat. Add the garlic and cook, stirring, for 1 minute, or until fragrant. Take care the garlic does not burn. Add the catsup, vinegar, pepper sauce, brown sugar, and mustard and stir to mix. Reduce the heat to low and cook, stirring occasionally, for about 10 minutes, or until thickened.

Try this traditional-style sauce with any grilled beef—particularly roast beef or plain, grilled steak.

Horseradish Cream Sauce

Makes about 1 cup

1 CUP HEAVY CREAM

4 TABLESPOONS PREPARED COMMER-
CIAL HORSERADISH

1 TEASPOON SUGAR

1 TEASPOON DISTILLED WHITE VINEGAR

1. Using an electric mixer, beat the cream in a large bowl on medium-high speed until soft peaks form.

2. Combine the horseradish, sugar, and vinegar in a separate bowl and stir well. Fold the cream into the horseradish mixture. Serve immediately. This sauce does not keep well.

Mushroom-Sage Sauce

Makes about 1 cup

½ OUNCE DRIED MUSHROOMS (SEE
NOTE)

1½ CUPS BOILING WATER

2 TABLESPOONS OLIVE OIL

2 TABLESPOONS CHOPPED FRESH SAGE

2 SHALLOTS, DICED

4 OUNCES FRESH CREMINI MUSH-
ROOMS, THINLY SLICED

4 OUNCES FRESH SHIITAKE MUSH-
ROOMS, STEMMED AND THINLY
SLICED

½ TEASPOON SALT

⅓ CUP HEAVY CREAM

1 TABLESPOON SHERRY

FRESHLY GROUND BLACK PEPPER TO
TASTE

1 TABLESPOON FINELY CHOPPED FLAT-
LEAF PARSLEY

1. Soak the dried mushrooms in a small bowl in the boiling water for 20 to 30 minutes. Drain the liquid into another bowl, straining it through a coffee filter to remove any sandy grit. Set the liquid aside. Gently squeeze the mushrooms to remove any excess liquid.

2. Heat the oil in a large skillet over medium-high heat. Add the sage and cook, stirring, for about 30 seconds, until sizzling and fragrant. Add the shallots and cook, stirring, for about 30 seconds, or until they begin to soften. Add the cremini and shiitake mushrooms, the reserved dried mushrooms, the reserved soaking liquid, and the salt. Stir until well mixed. Cover and cook for 3 or 4 minutes, or until the mushrooms are soft.

3. Add the cream and sherry to the skillet and season to taste with pepper. Bring to a simmer over medium-high heat and cook for 3 or 4 minutes or until the sauce is slightly thickened. Stir in the parsley and serve.

note: Dried mushrooms are sold in small amounts in most supermarkets. They may be a single type or a mixture of imported varieties and are sold in cellophane packages or plastic tubs. Any sort works here and adds deep, rich, earthy flavor.

A light, flavorful wine sauce is the perfect accompaniment for veal chops, but will enhance other mild grilled meats, too.

Merlot Wine Sauce   *Makes about 1 cup*

3 CUPS MERLOT OR CABERNET
   SAUVIGNON (OR ONE 750ML
   BOTTLE)
3 CUPS BEEF OR CHICKEN BROTH
1/4 CUP FINELY CHOPPED SHALLOTS
1 TABLESPOON CHOPPED FRESH THYME
   OR 1 TEASPOON DRIED THYME
1 TABLESPOON UNSALTED BUTTER
SALT AND FRESHLY GROUND BLACK
   PEPPER TO TASTE

1. Combine the wine, broth, shallots, and thyme in a nonreactive saucepan. Bring to a boil over high heat, reduce the heat, and simmer for 45 minutes to 1 hour until reduced to about $1^1/_2$ cups and the sauce has a thick, syrupy consistency. (The sauce may be made up to one day ahead to this point. Reheat before proceeding.)

2. Remove the sauce from the heat and whisk in the butter. Season with salt and pepper. Serve immediately.

This robust sauce perks up the flavor of game or beef.

Red Wine-Herb Sauce   *Makes about ³/₄ cup*

2 TABLESPOONS OLIVE OIL

³/₄ CUP SLICED LEEKS, WHITE PART
   ONLY

¹/₂ CUP THINLY SLICED ONIONS

¹/₂ CUP THINLY SLICED CARROTS

2 CLOVES GARLIC, CRUSHED

¹/₂ CUP COARSELY CHOPPED PARSLEY
   STEMS

1 TEASPOON CHOPPED FRESH THYME
   OR ¹/₂ TEASPOON DRIED THYME

¹/₄ TEASPOON BLACK PEPPERCORNS

¹/₈ TEASPOON FENNEL SEED

1 SMALL BAY LEAF

2 CUPS DRY RED WINE

1 TABLESPOON PORT WINE

4 TABLESPOONS UNSALTED BUTTER,
   SOFTENED

2 TABLESPOONS FINELY CHOPPED
   PARSLEY

FRESHLY GROUND BLACK PEPPER TO
   TASTE

1. Heat the oil in a nonreactive saucepan over medium heat. Add the leeks, onions, carrots, garlic, parsley, thyme, peppercorns, fennel, and bay leaf and cook, stirring, for about 5 minutes, or until the vegetables begin to soften. Add the wine, bring to a simmer over medium-high heat and cook for about 20 minutes, or until the vegetables are very soft.

2. Strain the sauce through a sieve, pressing on the solids with the back of a spoon to extract as much liquid as possible. You will have about ³/₄ cup of sauce. Discard the solids.

3. Return the sauce to the saucepan, add the port, and bring to a simmer. Cook for about 10 minutes until the sauce reduces to ¹/₂ cup.

4. With the pan set over medium-low heat, whisk in the butter, 1 tablespoon at a time. Make sure the each tablespoon is completely incorporated before adding the next. When the sauce is smooth and emulsified, stir in the parsley and season with pepper. Serve immediately.

Horseradish-Scallion Compound Butter

Makes about ¹/₂ cup

¹/₂ CUP (1 STICK) UNSALTED BUTTER,
  SOFTENED

1¹/₂ TABLESPOONS PREPARED COMMER-
  CIAL HORSERADISH

3 SCALLIONS, GREEN PARTS ONLY,
  CHOPPED

¹/₂ TEASPOON SALT

1. Using a hand-held electric mixer or in a mini food processor, blend the butter and horseradish until smooth. Add the scallions and salt and blend for about 1 minute longer, until fully incorporated. Alternatively, mix the ingredients by hand.

2. Lay a piece of plastic wrap on the countertop. Scrape the butter onto the plastic, and using the plastic wrap as a guide, form the butter into a log. Fold the ends closed and refrigerate until ready to use.

Gorgonzola-Scallion Compound Butter

Makes about 1 cup

1/2 CUP (1 STICK) UNSALTED BUTTER,
   SOFTENED

4 OUNCES GORGONZOLA CHEESE,
   CRUMBLED, AT ROOM TEMPERATURE

1/4 CUP CHOPPED SCALLIONS

1 TEASPOON COARSELY GROUND FRESH
   BLACK PEPPER

1/2 TEASPOON BALSAMIC VINEGAR

1. Using a hand-held electric mixer or in a mini food processor, blend the butter and gorgonzola until smooth. Add the scallions, pepper, and vinegar and blend for about 1 minute longer until fully incorporated. Alternatively, mix the ingredients by hand.

2. Lay a piece of plastic wrap on the countertop. Scrape the butter onto the plastic and using the plastic wrap as a guide, form the butter into a log. Fold the ends closed and refrigerate until ready to use.

Pesto, which originated in Italy, has become one of the best-loved uncooked sauces in America, and is particularly popular in the summer when aromatic fresh basil is plentiful. Serve this with burgers, alongside grilled chicken, or toss it with cooked pasta for a great summer side dish.

Summer Pesto   *Makes about 1 cup*

3 CUPS LOOSELY PACKED FRESH BASIL
    LEAVES
3 CLOVES GARLIC
1/2 CUP GRATED PARMESAN CHEESE
3 TABLESPOONS PINE NUTS
1/2 CUP EXTRA-VIRGIN OLIVE OIL
SALT AND FRESHLY GROUND BLACK
    PEPPER TO TASTE

1. Combine the basil, garlic, and cheese in a food processor and process just until ground. Add the pine nuts and process until the nuts are finely chopped.

2. With the processor running, add the olive oil through the feed tube in a steady stream until the oil is absorbed. Season with salt and pepper. Serve immediately or cover and refrigerate for up to 1 day. Stir before serving.

At times, mustard is more welcome on burgers than catsup or salsa. We like this on chicken and veal burgers.

Mustard Sauce   *Makes about ¹/₂ cup*

¹/₄ CUP DIJON MUSTARD

2 TABLESPOONS WHITE WINE VINEGAR

1 TABLESPOON SUGAR

1 TEASPOON DRY MUSTARD

¹/₄ CUP OLIVE OIL

1 TEASPOON HERBES DE PROVENCE
   (SEE NOTE)

Whisk together the mustard, vinegar, sugar, and dry mustard in a small bowl. Slowly add the olive oil, whisking constantly, until incorporated. Stir in the herbes de Provence. Serve immediately, or refrigerate for as long as 2 days. Whisk before serving.

note: Herbes de Provence are available in supermarkets, but if you cannot find them, use dried oregano or thyme, or a mixture of the two.

cross America, commercial salsas now outsell catsup. The word simply means "sauce" in Spanish and can be made with numerous ingredients. This one, made with fresh fruit and berries, and given a little kick by jalapeños, is really good with sweet meats, such as lamb and pork. But try it with burgers, too.

Minted Summer Fruit Salsa   *Makes about 2¼ cups*

1 CUP DICED STRAWBERRIES

1 CUP DICED MANGO

¾ CUP DICED KIWI

¼ CUP CHOPPED RED ONION

1 OR 2 JALAPEÑOS, SEEDED AND DICED

3 TABLESPOONS FRESH LIME JUICE

3 TABLESPOONS FINELY CHOPPED
   FRESH MINT

1 TEASPOON LIGHT BROWN SUGAR

Combine all the ingredients in a bowl and stir gently to blend. Serve immediately, or cover and refrigerate for several hours. Let the salsa reach room temperature before serving.

Mexicans are master salsa chefs and this condiment is based on the type that is served regularly in that sunny country. Tomatillos are sometimes called "Mexican" or "green tomatoes," although they are only distantly related to the common garden tomato. Small fruits covered with a papery husk that must be removed before use, tomatillos taste slightly acidic and herbal.

South-of-the-Border Tomatillo Salsa   *Makes about 2 cups*

8 TOMATILLOS (ABOUT ¾ POUND), HUSKED, WASHED, AND COARSELY CHOPPED

3 TABLESPOONS CHOPPED CILANTRO

2 TABLESPOONS CHOPPED SCALLIONS OR RED ONIONS

1 JALAPEÑO OR SERRANO CHILI, SEEDED AND CHOPPED

¼ CUP FRESH LIME JUICE

2 TABLESPOONS PEANUT OIL

½ TEASPOON SALT

SUGAR (OPTIONAL)

Combine the tomatillos, cilantro, scallions, chili, lime juice, oil, and salt in a glass or ceramic bowl and stir gently to mix. Adjust the seasonings, adding a little sugar if desired. Let the salsa stand for about 1 hour, allowing the flavors to blend. Serve or cover and refrigerate for as long as several hours. Let the salsa come to room temperature before serving.

This type of salsa, made with chopped tomatoes, bell peppers, and herbs, is a classic *salsa fresca*—which means it is not cooked. Serve this with just about any meat or poultry. We especially like it on burgers.

Baja-Style Tomato Salsa   *Makes about 2 cups*

1 POUND TOMATOES, CHOPPED

2 YELLOW OR RED BELL PEPPERS, SEEDED AND CHOPPED

1 CUP COOKED CORN KERNELS (SEE NOTE)

3 SCALLIONS, FINELY CHOPPED

2 JALAPEÑO OR SERRANO CHILIES, SEEDED AND CHOPPED

1 LARGE CLOVE GARLIC, MINCED

3 TABLESPOONS FINELY CHOPPED CILANTRO

1 TABLESPOON FRESH LIME JUICE

2 TEASPOONS CIDER VINEGAR

1/2 TEASPOON SALT, OR TO TASTE

Combine the tomatoes, peppers, corn, scallions, chilies, garlic, cilantro, lime juice, vinegar, and salt in a glass or ceramic bowl and stir gently to mix. Adjust the salt. Let the salsa stand for about an hour to let the flavors blend. Serve or cover and refrigerate for several hours. Let the salsa come to room temperature before serving.

note: You can use frozen corn kernels, cooked and cooled. For better flavor, use leftover boiled summer corn, or, best yet, grill a few ears over hot coals or roast them in a very hot oven (400°F.) until the husks blacken, which will take about 15 minutes and require turning several times. Let the corn cool and then slice the kernels from the cobs.

For those who like the richer, sweet flavor of grilled vegetables, this salsa is a real treat. The dried chilies make it nicely spicy. (Omit them if you prefer a milder condiment.) Try this with simple grilled chicken breasts, or use it to jazz up a burger or sirloin steak.

Hot, Hot, Hot Grilled Salsa *Makes about 2 cups*

VEGETABLE OIL COOKING SPRAY

4 OR 5 RED OR YELLOW TOMATOES

1 RED ONION, CUT INTO 4 THICK
   SLICES

1 TABLESPOON OLIVE OIL

2 OR 3 CLOVES GARLIC, MINCED

3 TABLESPOONS CHOPPED CILANTRO

2 TABLESPOONS CHOPPED FLAT-LEAF
   PARSLEY OR FRESH MINT

1 OR 2 DRIED *CHILE DE ARBOL* OR
   OTHER HOT DRIED CHILI, TOASTED
   AND SHREDDED (SEE NOTE)

½ TEASPOON SALT

FRESH LIME JUICE (OPTIONAL)

1. Prepare a charcoal or gas grill. Lightly spray the grill rack with vegetable oil cooking spray. The coals should be moderately hot.

2. Rub the tomatoes and onion slices with olive oil. Place the vegetables on the grill and grill for 3 to 5 minutes until the vegetables are well marked, but not soft. Turn them often with tongs. Set aside until cool enough to handle.

3. Combine the garlic, cilantro, parsley, and chili in a bowl. Coarsely chop the tomatoes and onion and add to the bowl. Add the salt and a splash of lime juice, if desired. Stir gently and let the salsa stand for about 1 hour to let the flavors blend. Serve, or cover and refrigerate until ready to serve. Let the salsa come to room temperature before serving.

note: To toast the chilies, place them in a dry skillet and cook over medium-high heat for about 1 minute, until lightly browned. When cool, wearing plastic gloves to protect your skin, remove the stems and seeds and tear or shred the chili with your hands. Be sure to wash your hands before touching sensitive areas, such as eyes and mouth. The chilies can burn! Depending on your preference and the heat of the chilies, use 1 or 2 chilies.

We developed this to accompany the Stuffed Holiday Turkey Burgers on page 29, but liked it so much we also serve it alongside grilled turkey cutlets and grilled chicken.

Chunky Cranberry Catsup   *Makes about 1¹/₂ cups*

¹/₂ CUP SUGAR

¹/₄ CUP CIDER VINEGAR

1¹/₂ TEASPOONS MUSTARD SEEDS

1 TEASPOON SALT

1 BAY LEAF

PINCH OF GROUND CLOVES

1¹/₂ CUPS FRESH CRANBERRIES (ABOUT 6 OUNCES)

¹/₄ CUP GOLDEN RAISINS

1 SHALLOT, MINCED

1. Combine the sugar, vinegar, mustard seeds, salt, bay leaf, and cloves in a nonreactive saucepan and bring to a boil over medium heat. Reduce the heat to medium-low and simmer for about 10 minutes.

2. Add the cranberries, raisins, and shallot and simmer, partially covered and stirring often, for about 15 minutes, or until most of the liquid evaporates and the catsup thickens. Let cool to room temperature and serve at room temperature or chilled. If not using immediately, cover and refrigerate for as long as 2 days.

This marinade is a classic combination of oil and vinegar, mustard and garlic. You can dress this marinade up to suit your own tastes, but it's just about perfect as it is and terrific for marinating flank steak, blade lamb chops, lamb riblets, or just about any red meat.

Red Wine Vinegar Marinade

Makes about 1³/₄ cups

1 CUP OLIVE OIL

¹/₂ CUP RED WINE VINEGAR

1 TABLESPOON WORCESTERSHIRE
   SAUCE

1 TABLESPOON DIJON MUSTARD

2 CLOVES GARLIC, CHOPPED

2 TABLESPOONS FINELY CHOPPED
   SCALLIONS

FRESHLY GROUND PEPPER TO TASTE

Whisk together all the ingredients in a glass or ceramic bowl until blended. Adjust the seasoning. Use according to the recipe, or cover and refrigerate for as long as 2 days.

We use a mixture of wine and wine vinegar in this elegant, easy marinade. Use it for chicken, veal, or any mild meat.

White Wine Marinade   *Makes about 1 cup*

½ CUP OLIVE OIL

¼ CUP DRY WHITE WINE

¼ CUP TARRAGON WHITE WINE
    VINEGAR

1 TABLESPOON CHOPPED FRESH
    TARRAGON OR CHERVIL

1 CLOVE GARLIC, MINCED

SALT AND FRESHLY GROUND BLACK
    PEPPER TO TASTE

Whisk together all the ingredients in a glass or ceramic bowl until blended. Adjust the seasonings. Use according to the recipe, or cover and refrigerate for as long as 2 days.

oasting spices enhances their flavors and this marinade, which combines some of the classic flavors of Asia, is wonderful on chicken, beef, pork—you name it.

Toasted Cumin Marinade *Makes about 1¹/₂ cups*

1 CUP CANOLA OIL

¹/₂ CUP FRESH LIME OR LEMON JUICE

1 TEASPOON TOASTED CUMIN SEEDS
   (SEE NOTE)

2 CLOVES GARLIC, CHOPPED

2 TABLESPOONS CHOPPED CILANTRO

SALT AND FRESHLY GROUND BLACK
   PEPPER TO TASTE

Whisk together all the ingredients in a glass or ceramic bowl until blended. Adjust the seasonings. Use according to the recipe, or cover and refrigerate for as long as 2 days.

note: To toast the cumin seeds, spread them in a dry skillet and toast them over medium-high heat, shaking the pan to prevent scorching, for 4 or 5 minutes, or until fragrant. Transfer the seeds to a plate to cool and stop the cooking.

This is an all-time favorite. We have recipes in the book that pair it with steak and with chicken, but it is great on pork, too.

Teriyaki Marinade *Makes about 2 cups*

- ½ CUP LOW-SODIUM SOY SAUCE
- ½ CUP DRY SHERRY
- ⅓ CUP CANOLA OIL
- 6 TABLESPOONS RICE WINE VINEGAR
- 1 TABLESPOON SESAME OIL
- ¼ CUP FIRMLY PACKED LIGHT OR DARK BROWN SUGAR
- 2 TABLESPOONS CHOPPED FRESH GINGER
- 4 SCALLIONS, SLICED
- 2 CLOVES GARLIC, MINCED

Combine the soy sauce, sherry, canola oil, vinegar, sesame oil, and sugar in a glass or ceramic bowl and whisk until the sugar dissolves. Add the ginger, scallions, and garlic and stir gently. Use according to the recipe, or cover and refrigerate for as long as 2 days.

Real maple syrup gives this fruity marinade just the sweetness it needs to enhance pork or chicken.

Maple Syrup Marinade *Makes about 1 ¹/₂ cups*

1 CUP APPLE CIDER OR UNSWEETENED APPLE JUICE

¹/₃ CUP CIDER VINEGAR

3 TABLESPOONS REAL MAPLE SYRUP

2 TABLESPOONS PREPARED COMMER-CIAL HORSERADISH

2 TEASPOONS WORCESTERSHIRE SAUCE

FRESHLY GROUND BLACK PEPPER TO TASTE

Whisk together all the ingredients in a glass or ceramic bowl until blended. Adjust the seasoning with pepper. Use according to the recipe, or cover and refrigerate for as long as 2 days.

note: If you prefer, substitute beer for the cider. The beer can be flat.

Dry rubs are one of the best-kept secrets of backyard chefs. They can be made in batches and stored in a plastic bag or small glass jar with the other spices in your cupboard. Rub them into the meat, refrigerate the meat, and let the rub draw the moisture from the center of the meat to the surface. The flavors penetrate the meat as it marinates in its own juices.

Peppery Dry Rub   *Makes a generous ¹/₂ cup*

3 TABLESPOONS CHILI POWDER

2 TABLESPOONS FRESHLY GROUND
   BLACK PEPPER

2 TABLESPOONS PAPRIKA

2 TEASPOONS CRUSHED RED PEPPER

1 TEASPOON SALT

1 CLOVE GARLIC, MINCED

Mix the ingredients together in a glass jar or bowl. Cover and shake to mix. Refrigerate until ready to use.

Dry rubs can be made with any of your favorite spices—think of our formulas as blueprints for your own creations. Don't be shy when using one. Rub it liberally over the meat.

Spicy Dry Rub *Makes about ¹/₃ cup*

2 TABLESPOONS CHILI POWDER

2 TABLESPOONS CAYENNE PEPPER

1 TABLESPOON GROUND CORIANDER

1 TEASPOON CRUSHED RED PEPPER

SALT AND FRESHLY GROUND BLACK
   PEPPER TO TASTE

Mix the ingredients together in a glass jar or bowl. Cover and shake to mix. Store in a cool dry place until ready to use.

When the meat is cooked, the dry rub, which has turned wet and sticky during marinating, becomes a delectable crust. This one is great on chicken and pork.

Sweet 'n Spicy Dry Rub   *Makes about ¹/₃ cup*

2 TABLESPOONS PACKED LIGHT OR
  DARK BROWN SUGAR
1 TABLESPOON FINELY CHOPPED
  GARLIC
1 TABLESPOON DRIED MARJORAM
1 TABLESPOON SALT
1 TABLESPOON FRESHLY GROUND
  BLACK PEPPER
¹/₂ TEASPOON CAYENNE PEPPER
¹/₄ TEASPOON GROUND ALLSPICE

Mix the ingredients together in a glass jar or bowl. Cover and shake to mix. Store in a cool dry place until ready to use.

Rub this heady paste into pork, lamb or chicken and let the meat marinate for a good long time—overnight is best. The scotch bonnet peppers give the seasoning a searing heat as well as a sweetly aromatic quality that together provide the characteristic Jamaican taste. Cook jerked meat long and slow over moderately hot or cooler coals.

Jerk Seasoning *Makes about 1 cup*

1/2 CUP FINELY CHOPPED ONIONS

1/3 CUP FINELY CHOPPED SCALLIONS
   (4 TO 6 SCALLIONS)

1/4 CUP FIRMLY PACKED FRESH THYME
   LEAVES AND TENDER STEMS

4 CLOVES GARLIC, FINELY CHOPPED

2 TABLESPOONS FRESH ORANGE JUICE

2 TABLESPOONS FRESH LIME JUICE

2 TABLESPOONS HOT PEPPER SAUCE
   (MADE FROM SCOTCH BONNETS OR
   HABANERO CHILIES, IF POSSIBLE) OR
   1 TO 3 SCOTCH BONNET OR
   HABANERO CHILIES, SEEDED AND
   MINCED, DEPENDING ON TASTE

1 TABLESPOON FINELY CHOPPED FRESH
   GINGER

2 TEASPOONS GROUND CORIANDER

2 TEASPOONS FRESHLY GROUND BLACK
   PEPPER

1 TEASPOON GROUND ALLSPICE

1 TEASPOON SALT

1/2 TEASPOON GROUND NUTMEG

1/2 TEASPOON GROUND CINNAMON

Combine all the ingredients in a small bowl and mix to form a coarse paste. Use immediately or transfer to a glass jar, cover, and refrigerate for as long as 1 month.

This is a classic rub with its roots in India, where the spices are ground together in a mortar with a pestle. Rub it into chicken, pork, or lamb.

Garam Masala   *Makes about ¹/₄ cup*

2 TABLESPOONS PLUS 2 TEASPOONS
  GROUND CARDAMOM
1 TABLESPOON GROUND CINNAMON
1 TEASPOON GROUND CLOVES
1 TEASPOON FRESHLY GROUND BLACK
  PEPPER
¹/₂ TEASPOON NUTMEG

Mix the ingredients together in a glass jar or bowl. Cover and shake to mix. Store in a cool, dry place until ready to use.

Lemongrass is an integral flavoring in all Southeast Asian cooking and has found its way into American greengrocers and supermarkets, as well as Asian markets. It tastes slightly lemony and so provides lovely flavor to many preparations. It is long, slender, and pale green, and may be sold trimmed or not.

Asian-Style Lemongrass Paste *Makes about 1 cup*

6 TABLESPOONS CHOPPED LEMON-
GRASS

3 TABLESPOONS FIRMLY PACKED
BROWN SUGAR

1 TABLESPOON PLUS 1 TEASPOON
MINCED FRESH GINGER

1 TABLESPOON PLUS 1 TEASPOON
CRACKED BLACK PEPPERCORNS

1 TABLESPOON MINCED GARLIC

1 TABLESPOON CUMIN SEEDS

Mix the ingredients together in a glass jar or bowl. Cover and shake to mix. Refrigerate until ready to use.

The addition of orange juice and water makes this more of a paste than a rub—although its texture lies somewhere between the two. It keeps for four or five days.

Curry Paste Rub   *Makes about ³/₄ cup*

VEGETABLE OIL COOKING SPRAY

¹/₂ CUP CURRY POWDER

2 TABLESPOONS CHOPPED FRESH
    GINGER

2 CLOVES GARLIC, CHOPPED

1¹/₂ TEASPOONS CRUSHED CORIANDER
    SEEDS

3 TABLESPOONS ORANGE JUICE

2 TABLESPOONS WATER

SALT TO TASTE

1. Lightly spray a small skillet with vegetable oil cooking spray. Combine the curry powder, ginger, garlic, and coriander seeds in the skillet and cook over medium-low heat, stirring, for 2 or 3 minutes until fragrant. Add the orange juice and water and stir gently until absorbed. The mixture will be dry and crumbly although it should hold together in a mass. Season with salt.

2. Use immediately or transfer the rub to a covered container and refrigerate until ready to use.

Prepared mayonnaise becomes a palette for numerous culinary possibilities. Season it with roasted garlic, roasted peppers, or chopped herbs, as we have in the following three recipes.

Roasted Garlic Mayonnaise

Makes about 1 cup

2 WHOLE HEADS GARLIC

1 TEASPOON OLIVE OIL

1 CUP PREPARED MAYONNAISE

1 TEASPOON LEMON JUICE

1. Preheat the oven to 400°F.

2. Remove loose, papery skin from the garlic heads but do not separate them into cloves. Cut off the top $1/2$ inch of each head. Rub each head with oil and wrap them in aluminum foil, making 2 packets. Set the packets on a baking sheet or in a baking dish and roast for 45 minutes to 1 hour until the garlic feels very soft when the packets are squeezed gently.

3. Unwrap the garlic heads and let cool.

4. Squeeze the garlic from the cloves and transfer the garlic to the bowl of a food processor. Pulse 3 or 4 times until smooth. Add the mayonnaise and lemon juice and process until smooth and well combined. Serve immediately, or cover and refrigerate for up to 2 days.

Roasted Red Pepper Mayonnaise

Makes about 1¹/₄ cups

2 ROASTED RED PEPPERS, SEEDED AND
  COARSELY CHOPPED (PAGE 203)
1 CLOVE GARLIC, COARSELY CHOPPED
1 CUP PREPARED MAYONNAISE
PINCH CAYENNE PEPPER

Combine the peppers and garlic in a food processor and process until smooth. Add the mayonnaise and cayenne and process just until combined. Serve immediately, or cover and refrigerate for up to 2 days.

Herbed Mayonnaise

Makes about 1 cup

1 CUP PREPARED MAYONNAISE

½ CUP FINELY CHOPPED FLAT-LEAF
   PARSLEY

2 TABLESPOONS FINELY CHOPPED
   FRESH THYME

2 TABLESPOONS FINELY CHOPPED
   FRESH TARRAGON

2 TEASPOONS DIJON MUSTARD

Combine all the ingredients in a bowl and stir until well mixed. Serve immediately, or cover and refrigerate for up to 2 days.

If a recipe calls for roasted peppers, follow this recipe through Step 3. Omit the oil, salt, and pepper and other flavorings. As an alternative, you may roast the peppers on the grill over a hot fire. To roast one or two peppers, skewer them on long-handled forks and char them over a gas flame. The key is to char the skin on all sides of the peppers and then to let the peppers steam during cooling—accomplished in a covered bowl, as described in the recipe, or in a paper bag with the top folded. Do not peel the peppers under running water. The water dilutes the flavor. And do not worry if some charred bits of skin remain on the peppers. Use your fingers and a knife for peeling, rubbing off the skin as much as peeling it for the best flavor and texture.

Roasted Red or Yellow Peppers in Oil

Makes 4 peppers

4 RED OR YELLOW BELL PEPPERS,
    HALVED, SEEDED AND TRIMMED
SALT AND FRESHLY GROUND BLACK
    PEPPER TO TASTE
2 OR 3 TABLESPOONS EXTRA-VIRGIN
    OLIVE OIL
BALSAMIC VINEGAR (OPTIONAL)
CAPERS (OPTIONAL)

1. Preheat the broiler. Line the broiling tray with foil.

2. Place the peppers, skin sides up, on the broiling tray. Broil for about 15 minutes, turning, or until the peppers are charred and blistered on all sides. Transfer to a bowl and cover the bowl with foil. Set aside to steam and cool for about 15 minutes.

3. Rub the charred skin from the peppers and cut the peppers into the size needed for a recipe, or if serving as a side dish, cut into wide strips.

4. Place the peppers on a platter and season with salt and pepper. Drizzle with olive oil. If desired, splash with vinegar and sprinkle with capers.

Cuts of Meat

Throughout the book, we have taken care to explain which cuts of meat are best for different recipes, due to their qualities of size, tenderness, and composition. On the next pages are diagrams for beef, veal, lamb, and pork, to show the placement of the different cuts of meat. This could help you when you are buying meat—historically there have been different names for particular cuts of meat. While this is generally no longer true, familiarizing yourself with these charts might help you when speaking with your butcher.

Beef

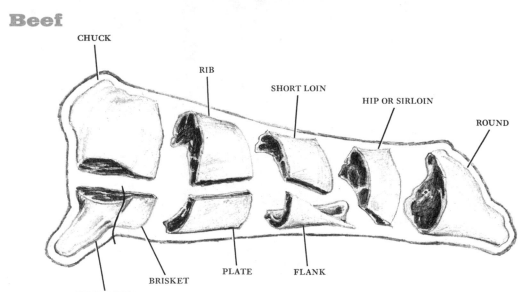

CHUCK

RIB

SHORT LOIN

HIP OR SIRLOIN

ROUND

FORESHANK

BRISKET

PLATE

FLANK

Beef carcass, divided into wholesale (primal) cuts.

Veal

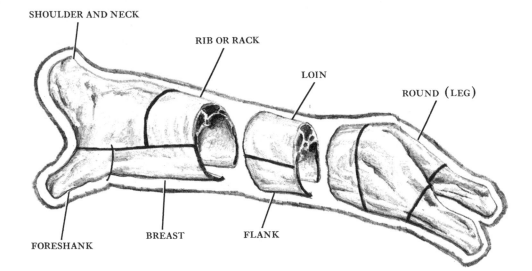

SHOULDER AND NECK

RIB OR RACK

LOIN

ROUND (LEG)

FORESHANK

BREAST

FLANK

Veal carcass, divided into wholesale (primal) cuts.

Lamb

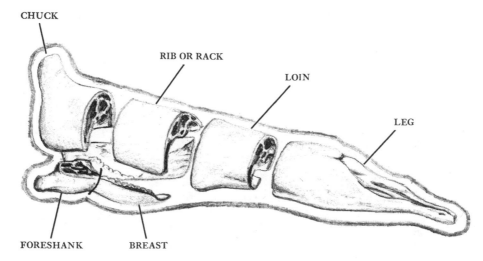

Lamb carcass, divided into wholesale (primal) cuts.

Pork

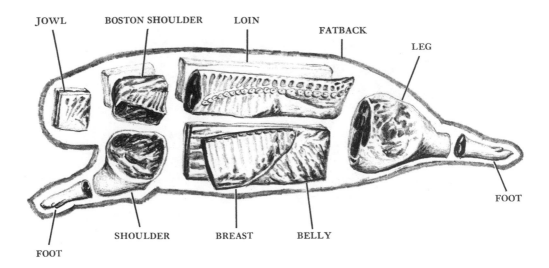

Pork carcass, divided into wholesale (primal) cuts.

Index

Garlic

and Cumin, Butterflied Leg of Lamb with, 78

Mayonnaise, Roasted, 200

-Roasted Chicken, Ten-Clove, 131

Garlicky

Grilled Eggplant, Classic Grilled Butterflied Leg of Lamb with, 74

Grilled Short Ribs, 63

gas grills

convenience of, 2–3

features of, 3

indirect heat for (special instructions), 6

thermometers in, 8

Ginger-Lemongrass Chicken, Southeast Asian, 126

Gingery Chicken, 117

Glazed

Corned Beef, Grilled, 61

Sweet-and-Sour Chicken Wings, 125

Goat Cheese and Black Pepper, Grilled Chicken (breasts) with, 134

Gorgonzola-Scallion Compound Butter, 180; Grilled Filet Mignon with, 41

Grape and Pork Kabobs with Sweet-Sour Sauce, 102

Grapefruit and Chipotle Marinade, Grilled Duck Breast in, with Grapefruit-Avocado Salad, 159

gray ash, 7. *See also* fuel for grilling

Greek Lamb Burgers, 23

Green Chili Sauce, Grilled Sirloin Steak with, 43

grilling. *See also* fuel for grilling

basics of, 1–9

direct and indirect heat, 5–6

equipment for, 8–9

flip-flop method, 36

heat of fire for (hot, moderately hot, etc), 6–7; chart, 7; icons for, 7

internal temperature for meat and poultry, 8

lighting coals for, 4–5

skewers for, bamboo or metal, 73

grills, types of, 2–3

brazier-style, 2

covered (inexpensive), 2

gas, 2–3; advantages of, 3

hibachis (Japanese-style brazier), 2

how to choose, 1

how to clean, 9

kettle-style, 2

racks for, 13

ground meat, 14. *See also* Name of Meat (Beef, Chicken, Lamb, Pork, Turkey, Veal)

about freezing, 13; refrigerating, 13

grinding your own, 14

H

Hamburger. *See also* Beef Burgers

about cuts of beef for, 15

Classic, 15

meat (*cont.*)

    leftovers, 113

    refrigeration of, 72

Meat Loaf, Grilled, 65

Mediterranean Grilled Chicken Salad, 140

Merlot Wine Sauce, 177

mesquite wood chips, for flavor, 4

Mint-Brushed Lamb Chops, 79

Minted Summer Fruit Salsa, 183

"moderately cool" coals, 6–7; chart, 7; icons for, 7

"moderately hot" coals, 6–7; chart, 7; icons for, 7

"moderately hot to hot" coals, 6–7; chart, 7; icons for, 7

Moroccan-Style Rock Cornish Game Hens, Grilled, 146

Mushroom(s)

    -Bacon Burger, 19

    Grilled Stuffed, Lamb Chops with, 80–81

    -Sage Sauce, 176

    and Scallions, Grilled, Grilled Steak Salad with, 48

    Stuffed Cheeseburger Deluxe, 18

    and Veal Brochettes with Fresh Sage, 67

    -Veal Burgers, 21

Mustard

    and Bourbon, Pork Tenderloin Rubbed with, 93

    Duck Breast, Grilled, with Cracklings, 157

-Glazed Shoulder Lamb Chops, 83

and Herb Marinade, Rabbit with, 167

-Honey Chicken Kabobs, 136

Sauce, 182

-Thyme Crusted Flank Steak, 54

N

New York strip. *See* Shell Steak

O

Olivada and Rosemary, Grilled Chicken Breast Rolls with, 135

Onions, Grilled, Blue Cheese Burgers with, 17

open-hand test to test heat of coals, 7

Orange Sauce, Pheasant with, 162

outdoor grill, equipment for, 8–9

P

pastes and rubs, dry, 170. *See also* Rubs

Pears, Grilled Curried, Pork Kabobs with, 104

Pepper Jack Cheese Burgers, 16

Peppers, Roasted Red or Yellow, in Oil, 203

Peppery

    Chicken Wings, 124

    Dry Rub, 193

Pesto

    Butter, Prosciutto and Fontina, Turkey Roulades with, 150

    Summer, 181